Born and raised in Art, Mason County, Texas, Gilbert J. Jordan received his A.B. from Southwestern University, George-town, Texas. He earned his M.A. from the University of Texas, Austin, and his Ph.D. from Ohio State University. Emeritus professor of German at Southern Methodist University, he has published many works on German language and literature.

Yesterday in the
Texas Hill Country

By

GILBERT J. JORDAN

Foreword by
TERRY G. JORDAN

Texas A&M University Press
COLLEGE STATION AND LONDON

Copyright © 1979 by Gilbert J. Jordan

Library of Congress Cataloging in Publication Data

Jordan, Gilbert John, 1902–
    Yesterday in the Texas hill country.

    Bibliography: p.
    Includes index.
    1. German Americans—Texas—Mason Co.—Social
life and customs. 2. Jordan family. 3. Jordan, Gilbert
John, 1902. 4. Methodists in Mason Co., Tex. 5. German
Americans—Texas—Mason Co.—Biography. I. Title.
F392.M36J67   976.4'62'00431   78-21774
ISBN 0-89096-067-4

Manufactured in the United States of America
FIRST EDITION

To my parents
Daniel and Emilie Jordan

Contents

List of Illustrations

Foreword

Texas offers much to anyone interested in traditional farm and ranch life, for the state is culturally diverse, a mosaic colored by a variety of ethnic groups. Even the headlong rush of Texans to the cities, to the industrial-urban Promised Land, has not altogether obliterated the many rural ways of life. In vestige, at least, these traditional life-styles and folkways survive. But we have lost much in the last half-century, and we are about to lose much more. The practitioners of traditional rural ways are aging; those who would have been the perpetuators have fled to the cities. Voluntarily and collectively, rapidly and indiscriminately, our people are forsaking the ways of their fathers and mothers. A generation gap is widening into a cultural chasm. All too soon the traditional rural Texas will be gone.

Some living among us have lived two lives, one on either side of the chasm. Born and raised in pre-electric, pre-automobile, rural Texas, they crossed bridges burned long ago to join the urban culture. My father, Gilbert J. Jordan, is such a person. His roots are among the German Methodist ranch folk of the Texas Hill Country. "German Methodists"—the very term seems self-contradictory. Discard all your stereotyped images of Germans, for these are, unlikely as it may seem, teetotaling Teutons who renounced dancing and belonged to no social or recreational clubs, who embraced pietistic Methodism with a fervor rarely found among Anglo-Texans. My father chose to leave this subculture as a young man and became a university professor. Several years ago, I encouraged him to write his reminiscences of ranch life among the German Methodists during the first quarter of the century. This book is the result of my request.

My motives in asking him were both selfish and professional. City-born and city-raised, I desired to know more about my rural cultural heritage, about these curious Germans whose influence I saw so clearly marked on my own personality and tastes. More important, I wanted a record for posterity of this unique and interesting ethnic-religious minority and their way of life. Field research for my own doctoral dissertation and frequent contacts with my elderly German-American relatives in Mason County warned me that this way of life was rapidly dying. Largely undocumented and unknown to most Texans, Methodist German ranch life would soon be gone and forgotten. My father was, I felt, particularly qualified to capture in prose the last decades when Teutonic cultural traits, pleasingly mixed with American customs, flourished in the semiarid hills of west-central Texas. I could not write the account, for I had never been a part of this subculture, nor could my elderly kinfolk, for they lacked the writing skills and the needed perspective of an outsider. Only my father had lived the two lives necessary to the authorship. Now, thanks to his efforts, we can all live on a Hill Country ranch among German Methodists early in the twentieth century. And we can lament the passing of this unique way of life.

TERRY G. JORDAN
North Texas State University

Preface

IN a magazine article entitled "Milestones and Stumbling Blocks," Fred B. Kniffen, who is of my age-group, wrote: "I assert that in my childhood I lived closer to the ways of my great-grandparents . . . than to those of my grandchildren of today, and hence many of my boyhood ways and experiences were those of the pioneers." So it was in my family and in countless others. It is this life of an earlier day to which I am returning and about which I am writing. I was prompted by the celebration of the 1976 Bicentennial of the United States of America and by the renewed interest in the early days of our country, as well as the recent concern over the various ethnic cultures and their contributions to the sum total of our American civilization. Thus I write about people of earlier generations and how they lived in houses without modern conveniences; how they rode in buggies, hacks, and wagons; how they shopped in small-town stores; what they did in church and school; how they produced, preserved, and prepared their food; how they worked on farms and ranches; what the early artisans accomplished without the aid of modern technology; and what life was like in a bilingual community. The present book is a portrayal of the world of my childhood in the first quarter of our century, and a record of a way of life long past and in part forgotten or unknown.

Much has been written about the German settlements in Texas and the contributions of the German element to the state and to the various towns and counties. However, very little has been said about life in the homes, schools, churches, and communities of the German groups. This is particularly true of the German Methodists, who constitute a sort of separatist group in the German Belt of Texas. To fill this vacuum and to bridge the ethnic and generation gap, I set myself the task of relating the impressions of my youth in a small community in the rural, German–Texas Hill Country.

For the most part, I relied on my own memory and research for the material presented here in an effort to give the true flavor of life among my people. I searched diligently for *Kulturerbe* ("cultural heritage"), both English and German, like songs, poems, ditties, riddles, sayings, stories, games, and prayers, and interspersed this material in the narrative. Many of the quotations are a part of our common Anglo-American tradition, but many are German and belong to the German–Texas Hill Country heritage. Whenever I quote any material in German, I always add English translations, usually my own, most of them in English verse.

Many people, especially members of my own family, supplied me with information that supplemented or verified my own recollections. Through questionnaires and personal interviews, I gathered more subject matter than I could possibly use. My brothers and sisters and their spouses (Frank and Ella Jordan, Dan and Dina Jordan, Hulda Jordan Donop, Olga Jordan Schulze, and Emily Jordan Mood), my wife (Vera Tiller Jordan), several cousins (Ervin Jordan and John H. Kothmann) and friends (Anne and Mary Wight, Waltraud Bartscht, and Kate C. Warnick), and others too numerous to mention here, gave useful facts and suggestions as the work began to take shape. The most valuable assistance came from my son, Terry G. Jordan, who not only urged me to write my account but also read the manuscript carefully, made many significant suggestions, and prepared the map for chapter 1. His influence is present in various sections of the book. My special thanks go to my former student, William A. Owens, whose books like *This Stubborn Soil* and *A Fair and Happy Land*, among others, inspired me, and who suggested many improvements in my book.

Some of the material of the present volume has appeared in essay form elsewhere and is presented here with the permission of the publishers concerned. Chapter 5, "Sunday Meant Church," contains subject matter treated in an article, "Texas German Methodism in a Rural Setting," *Perkins Journal* 31, (Spring, 1978): 1–21; and chapter 9, "Hundred Years of Texas German," is adapted from my essay "The Texas German Language of the Western Hill Country," *Rice University Studies* 63 (Summer, 1977): 59–71.

YESTERDAY IN THE TEXAS HILL COUNTRY

From Peasant to Pioneer

THE story of the German settlement of Texas has been told so often by learned writers that it does not need to be repeated here, at least not in detail. Suffice it to say that I am descended from German peasant farmers who were attracted to Texas by the exaggerated promise that a land of milk and honey awaited them here and that they could easily establish a new Canaan in the Promised Land. The mass movement of Germans to Texas in the 1840's was sponsored by a group of German petty nobles who organized an emigration society, the Mainz Society of Nobles, also known as the Society for the Protection of German Immigrants in Texas. This immigration company contracted with the Republic of Texas to bring German settlers to the large Fisher-Miller land grant located between the upper Colorado and the Llano rivers. The nobles hoped to get rich by this colonization scheme and at the same time to help ambitious peasant farmers escape from overpopulated rural Germany. Some say the nobles even envisioned Texas as an overseas colony under their rule. In almost every respect, the nobles failed. Within a few years their Texas colonization project had gone bankrupt, and the annexation of Texas by the United States in 1845 had ended their hopes for an overseas empire. But before failing, the Society of Nobles had brought my ancestors and some seven thousand other Germans to the state.

My immigrant ancestors were in many respects like the generations of peasants in Germany who, for hundreds of years before them, had farmed the land and practiced some modest cottage handicraft. Both of my immigrant grandfathers had acquired such skills to supplement their farming activity. Ernst Jordan was a linen weaver in Wehrstedt, Hannover, and Anton Willmann worked as a cabinet-maker and wheelwright in Rauschwitz, Silesia. The German economic and social system of the mid-nineteenth century placed a low ceiling on their potential for achievement, and the males faced lengthy service in the military. Unlike their forefathers, who had for centuries been tenant serfs bound to the soil, they had attained freedom and a modest landownership. Their appetite for economic and social advancement had been whetted, yet Germany offered no real hope for further progress. They should not be viewed as poverty-stricken and uneducated. They had modest amounts of hard cash put aside in hiding places in their substantial farmhouses, and they had learned the basic skills taught in their village schools. And, unlike their forefathers since feudal times, they were free to leave and seek their fortune in another land.

To these recently freed, newly literate peasants, the noblemen of the Society offered a chance of escape, a chance to amount to something and to continue to improve their economic position. "Come with us to America, to Texas," the nobles said, "and there you can prosper, there your hard work will be rewarded." The more ambitious among the peasants, the more adventurous, could not resist so tempting an invitation, and they left their tight-knit farm villages and lush, green countryside, their ancient ancestral homes, their kith and kin, and came to Texas as pioneers.

They found in Texas no land of milk and honey. Instead of the Eden described in the advertising brochures of the Society of Nobles they encountered hunger, cholera, malaria, dysentery, drought, hostile Indians, poisonous snakes, and a hundred other hazards. But in time they did, indeed, prosper. By the time I was born in 1902, my people had acquired land by the thousands of acres, cattle by the hundreds, and a respected social and economic position in the community. The old German adage concerning the slow progress of immigrants, *dem Ersten Tod, dem Zweiten Not, dem Dritten Brot* ("for the first generation, death; for the second, deprivation; for the third, bread"), did not apply in our case. My immigrant grandfather Ernst Jordan passed through all these stages in one lifetime. Death he witnessed in his first four years in Texas when his wife died on the Indianola beach, his first-born child perished in the New Braunfels epidemics, and his second wife succumbed to disease at Fredericksburg. He himself had to overcome sickness and hunger in these early years. Death was his almost daily companion in 1849, when he had the task of conveying the dead to the Fredericksburg cemetery in his wagon drawn by two black oxen. Deprivation he knew from 1850 to 1870, the hard years when he established a family and a Mason County ranch. "Bread" he enjoyed in abundance for the last twenty years of his life, as he attained the prosperity he had left Germany to seek.

During the first ten years in Texas, from 1845 to the mid-1850's, most of my ancestors, the Jordans and the Bickenbachs, lived in Fredericksburg. This settlement, like New Braunfels, was planned as a way station to the Fisher-Miller Grant across the Llano River, where each of these colonist families held 640 acres in land grants. However, in the 1840's it was impossible to move any farther both because the immigration society went bankrupt and because the Indians were still an ever-present danger.

The settlement of Fredericksburg was laid out on a farming plan similar to that of the German villages from which the immigrants had come. Each family received a town lot and a ten-acre plot of land nearby. This may have seemed to the newcomers an excellent arrangement, because a ten-acre plot was a large farm judged by the size of the landholdings they were familiar with in Germany. These settlers soon discovered, however, that such a small tract of land in this semiarid Hill Country was totally inadequate, and the people were faced with starvation. To eke out a meager living, they had to supplement the small-scale farming with additional enterprises or wages. Cattle raising on the open range was the best choice available, but the German peasants were unfamiliar with ranching, and it took time to acquire herds of cattle. The more resourceful settlers tried other ways of making a living, at least temporarily.

My grandfather Ernst Jordan acquired a wagon and some oxen and became a teamster. Although this was a new occupation for him, he knew from his experiences in Germany how to handle oxen. In Germany the oxen were usually controlled by a driver on foot, and Ernst knew how to do this, but in Texas he learned to drive his oxen by the English commands, calling out "gee" for a right turn, "haw" for a left, "get up" for "go ahead," and "whoa" for a signal to stop. He made long, slow trips, hauling goods from the coastal plains to the towns and frontier forts in the Hill Country.

When the starvation period was over in 1849, he married Lisette

Bickenbach. Together the couple saved every dollar they could spare and bought a section of land across the Llano River, on the Willow Creek, in present Mason County. This was a more favorable spot than the original land grant in San Saba County. They sold the original grant, and in 1856 they, along with the Hoersters and Kothmanns, moved to their Promised Land and began a new life in log cabins. Many others, almost all of them German Methodists, joined in this exodus from Fredericksburg.

After the move across the Llano, cattle raising and farming became Ernst's chief occupation. He brought a small herd of cattle along from Fredericksburg and began all over again with open-range cattle raising. But because this business did not become very profitable until after the Civil War, he also continued his hauling and teamster activity for some years, work in which his oldest son, Peter, joined him.

Once the cattle trails were opened in the 1860's, ranching became more profitable. Soon Ernst and his sons went on the big roundups two times each year to brand the calves and sell or consign cattle to the drovers who took large herds on the cattle trails to the railheads in Kansas. But he knew things would change before long. He said, "Es wird hier mal anders" ("Things will change here someday"), and he fenced in his original landholdings with rail and rock fences. As soon as he saved up some money, he bought more land, until he had about seven thousand acres and, beginning in 1883, he fenced it in, for the most part with barbed wire. This much land would have been nothing short of a principality in Europe. Not bad for a person who had begun his adult life as a landless peasant! In 1884 there was some fence cutting by people who wanted to keep open-range grazing, but this did not last long. Soon most of the ranches in the county were fenced in.

My great-grandparents Daniel Bickenbach and his wife Sophie Willach, together with their three younger children, Peter, Wilhelm, and Friederika, also joined in the Methodist move toward Mason, but they did not cross the Llano River; they settled instead at some distance to the south of the river near present Hilda. Here they helped establish a small community named, significantly, Canaan. It certainly was no "Promised Land," though, because it lay on choice Indian hunting and hiding grounds. After several years, life became so dan-

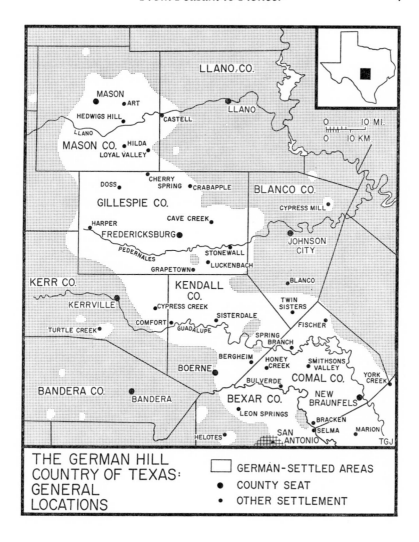

THE GERMAN HILL
COUNTRY OF TEXAS:
GENERAL
LOCATIONS

GERMAN-SETTLED AREAS
COUNTY SEAT
OTHER SETTLEMENT

gerous here, because of Indian raids and killings, that the family
moved to the town of Mason.

Anton Willmann and his wife Christina Niess, ancestors on my
mother's side, did not come to Texas until the 1850's. They first
settled on a farm at Bracken near New Braunfels, and thirty years
later, in 1883, they bought a small ranch and farm in Mason County
and moved to the new place.

It is significant that all my forebears were German-Methodist
ranching folk. To the outlander the words *German, Methodist,* and
ranch will seem curious companions at best, perhaps even completely
incongruous. It is not easy to envision a Central-European people
who adopted an Anglo-American religion and an Hispanic-Mexican
livestock economy. When I was a child growing up in this subculture,
however, I certainly had no sense of the uniqueness of my people.
Only later, when I left home and came into contact with other life-
styles, did I begin to realize how unusual my upbringing had been.

Being German or Texas-German did not make my family all
that distinctive. Much of south-central Texas was settled by German
immigrants. Our uniqueness lay more in our adherence to Methodism, a sect hardly known in Germany. Those immigrants who
came to Texas directly from Germany around the middle of the nineteenth century were Lutherans, Catholics, and reformed Evangelicals
—certainly not Methodists. Within a few years, however, some of the
newly arrived settlers were won over to the Methodists through the
ardent endeavors of missionaries, partly because there were not
enough Lutheran ministers and Catholic priests available to serve the
religious needs of the people on the Hill Country frontier. German-
speaking missionaries from the new German Methodist Church, organized in 1838 in Cincinnati, Ohio, came in by way of Louisiana
and filled the spiritual vacuum for some of the people. Their preaching appealed to the pietistic immigrants. The founder of the church
was Dr. Wilhelm Nast from Württemberg, Germany, who was converted to Methodism in America under the Reverend Wilbur Fisk.

My people were won over to Methodism in the early 1850's in
Fredericksburg, where they lived during the decade of 1846 to 1856.
The Reverend Eduard Schneider came by way of the German Methodist missions in Galveston, Victoria, and New Braunfels to preach
with Methodist fervor in Fredericksburg during the late 1840's. He

organized a Methodist church there and served as the first pastor from 1849 to 1851. Initially the people worshiped in the communal coffee-mill building used by all denominations as a church and by the entire community for school and civic purposes. Schneider was succeeded by the Reverend Charles A. Grote, who served as pastor from 1851 to 1855. During his ministry a new building was erected, the First Methodist Episcopal Church, South. My grandfather Ernst Jordan helped haul stones for the building and aided in the construction of the sanctuary.

While serving his first appointment there, Brother Grote made frequent horseback trips to the Llano River Valley, some thirty miles to the north, where a few German families had settled. Perhaps Grote began to think in terms of a German-Methodist Zion, an isolated region where the German converts could settle and raise their families in rural solitude. In any case, a mass migration of German Methodists from Fredericksburg to the Llano Valley was soon under way, and the Reverend Grote joined them. In 1856 he organized the Llano Valley Circuit. The original member churches were at Upper Willow Creek (later named Plehweville and then Art), Castell, Lower Willow Creek, and Hilda. My grandparents, Ernst and Lisette Jordan, as well as the Bickenbachs, were among the sixty-three charter members of this Llano Valley Circuit.

Some interesting tales are told about the Reverend Grote and his devotion to the work of the church. On a ride in 1852 from Fredericksburg to the Llano Valley, Grote encountered three heavy thunderstorms that would have turned back most men. When he arrived at the south bank of the river at Castell, the stream was at flood stage, and he had to spend the night sleeping on his saddle blanket spread out on the wet ground. The next morning the anxious people who had gathered for the Sunday services on the north side of the river saw him and sent some friendly Indians to bring him across on a horse. Since Grote could not swim and did not wish to ride on a swimming horse, the Indians signaled to him to hold on to the horse's tail and kick with his feet. Then one Indian swam ahead and led the horse, while two others swam along to the right and left of the parson.

Finally they reached an island near the other side of the river, and here they rested. Grote had swallowed so much water during several involuntary baptizings that he could not go on like this any farther. The Indians then stretched a rope from a tree on the island to a tree on the bank of the river and piloted the preacher to land. Grote promptly changed to borrowed clothes and preached his sermon in German under a large live-oak tree. His text was, "Ihr müsset von neuem geboren werden" ("Ye must be born again"). Even before he finished, the people fell on their knees and begged God for forgiveness and guidance.

This meeting under the live-oak tree was the first public worship on the Llano and it set the tone and pattern for the typical services of the Llano Valley Circuit. Later Grote became the pastor at Castell and of the entire circuit. He held devotionals in the homes of the people, just as he had done earlier while he was the preacher in Fredericksburg.

Entirely Methodist from the beginning, the Llano Valley of eastern Mason County and western Llano County has remained to the present day the most purely Methodist area in all of Texas. Mormon-like, my people came to the wilderness and created an isolated religious enclave. Brother Grote was their Brigham Young. The movement spread rapidly, and by the turn of the century there were eight congregations in the Llano River Circuit, and the whole valley was soon inundated in Teutonic Wesleyanism.

These rural churches were extremely evangelical and conservative. Most of the people lived by strict rules of morality and expected all others to do likewise. The old church books record in minute detail all the transactions, even trivia, that took place at the Quarterly Conferences. Members were sometimes reprimanded for irregular church attendance and threatened with expulsion. More serious deviations called for church trials, which are carefully recorded in the handwritten record books. In one case a member was tried for having an affair with a neighbor's wife; he was expelled from the church and forced to make a confession and do penance in the presence of the entire congregation before he was readmitted to membership. In spite of such incidents and some deviant behavior, the religious life prospered, and the people were known for their devotion to the church and its teachings. In the long run the people were more successful in preserving their religious heritage than their German language and other ethnic qualities.

Grandfather Ernst Jordan died on December 23, 1892, ten

years to the day before I was born. The prosperity he had won was still ours, though we had to work hard to maintain it, for the Texas Hill Country does not yield wealth easily. Mine is thus not a story of pioneering, although my life was still influenced by the pioneer spirit. My story is rather about the first and second generations of Texas-born, about the comfortable existence in the brief, pleasant interlude between the passing of the frontier and the coming of the machine age.

2

Home on the Willow Creek

THE little community where I grew up was Plehweville, but do not look for it on a map, at least not a modern one. First of all, it is too small to appear on most maps, and in addition its name has been changed. It was known as Upper Willow Creek, or *Oberwillow Creek*, to my immigrant grandparents, and as Plehweville to my parents and to my generation. Then in 1920 it was rechristened Art. We did not favor this change, no matter how arty the new name was, but we knew from experience how hard it was to spell the word which was derived from the first postmaster's name, Otto von Plehwe. People came up with all kinds of original orthographies, like Pleweville, Plehverville, Plehwerville, Pleeverville, Plehviville, Pleveville, Plewerville, Phlewerville, Phlehwerville, or some other of the many possible variations that any ingenious speller can devise. And then, too, the name was often confused with Pflugerville near Austin, so the Post Office Department wanted to change the name. My cousin Eli Dechert, the postmaster at that time, suggested Dechert. When the Washington bureaucrats asked for a shorter name, somebody came up with the impossible abbreviation Ert, and this led to the name Art. Washington seemed satisfied until someone discovered that "Art" was similar to "Arp" in east Texas. Although another Plehweville-Pflugerville confusion was threatened, no further changes were proposed, and the people had to live with the Art-Arp mix-up. You cannot win for losing in such matters. For a long time the people continued to call the little spot Plehweville, and the church was known as the *Oberwillow Creek Kirche*.

In this valley of the Willow Creek my ancestors had a major environmental adjustment to make. Removed three thousand miles from the beautiful green landscape of the Fatherland and set down in the semiarid ranch land of the Texas Hill Country, they must surely have felt distress. In one harassed generation, they made the enormous environmental transition from humid lands to dry, from cool to hot. This land must have looked strange to them indeed. Instead of their accustomed verdant, fertile countryside and rainy, cool climate, they found a drought-plagued, rocky land. The native vegetation they encountered gave warning of drought, even to the untrained eye of a displaced German. The spiny yucca plants, twisted mesquites, prickly-pear cactus, and thorny algerita bushes all spoke of semi-aridity. But as solace there were abundant oaks in the pastures and fine pecans along the Willow Creek. Tall grasses grew among the scattered trees, bushes, and outcroppings of granite, and the Willow Creek area was soon recognized as good cattle country.

The year 1856, when my ancestors arrived in Mason County, was one of the driest, so they probably were under no illusions about its climatic character. They knew, as did my generation, that in some years this country belonged to the Great American Desert to the west, while in others it was claimed by the humid east. The Willow Creek was dry when they first saw it, and even the rock-strewn Llano River, a few miles to the south, was only a trickle. The same stream the Reverend Grote had struggled so mightily to cross in the flood a few years earlier was easily passed over by their ox wagon laden with people and possessions.

Plehweville is not exactly a town, or even a village or hamlet. It is, rather, a scattering of buildings and houses, lacking any focal point other than the Willow Creek, the store, and the two churches. The store, which also contained the post office, is a short distance east of the creek on the north side of the Mason-Llano road, while our southern Methodist Church and graveyard are a quarter-mile away on a rise west of the creek and south of the road. The northern Methodists had their house of worship near the store and their cemetery a half-mile east from there. This northern Methodist Church was moved later, but the schoolhouse still stands a quarter-mile south of the store and the road, near the east bank of the Willow Creek. A visitor passing through Plehweville would scarcely have noticed the school's existence because it was so small and hidden among trees.

The dwellings and ranchsteads of the Plehweville residents were even more scattered than the public buildings. Few people lived within sight of each other. Our ranch was about two miles south of the church, on the dirt road to Fredericksburg, which paralleled the west bank of Willow Creek. South of us were the Standkes, and to our east and south, the Donops. Unlike most citizens of Plehweville, the Donops were descended from the German nobility. They had come to Texas as the university-educated von Donops, but by my time they were simply ranch folk like the rest of us. Downstream on the Willow Creek and near the Llano River lived other German settlers, such as the Martins, the Steinmanns, the Pluennekes, the Lehmbergs, and the Leifestes. Two or three miles east of the Plehweville store were the Eckerts. The old Kothmann house, a typical half-timbered German structure, stood just south of the store, though by my time most of the Kothmanns resided east and northeast of Plehweville and across the Llano River. The Hoersters owned the land stretching northeast from the store. To the northwest and along the upper reaches of Willow Creek, were Dannheim, Willmann, Jordan, Vater, and Hasse ranches, and farther west lived Grotes, Guenterts, Jordans, and Hoersters. Mr. Otto von Plehwe, and later Ernst Dannheim, owned the store and lived beside it.

A greater contrast to the tightly clustered farm villages of Germany can scarcely be imagined. It must surely have been a traumatic experience when my immigrant ancestors settled on isolated ranchsteads after having been accustomed to frequent contacts with neighbors in European villages or even Fredericksburg. To adjust to dispersed dwellings was difficult for them, particularly since the change occurred simultaneously with their adjustments to a new religion, a new livelihood, a strange environment, and a new culture and language, not to mention the occasional Anglo opposition to these "damn Dutch" immigrants. The anti-German prejudice was especially bitter during the Civil War and World War I, when there was persecution of German settlers.

During the Civil War there were confrontations between secessionists and German Unionists. To be sure, some of the German settlers in Texas, especially those in Comal County and the eastern part of the German Belt, fought with the Confederate armies, just as the earlier German immigrants had joined the Anglos in the Texas War of Independence and the Mexican-American War. Yet it is true there was some Unionist sympathy among the German settlers, especially in Kendall and Gillespie counties. As a result, Germans in general were persecuted as Union sympathizers, and some were lynched. In the Nueces River massacre, a group of German Union volunteers on their way to the North via Mexico were slain, and their bodies left unburied. Much later, after the bitter feelings of the war were calming down, the people of Comfort gathered the bones, buried them in their town, and put up a monument with the inscription *Treue der Union* ("Loyal to the Union"). Most of the German settlers were not involved in such dangerous encounters, but there was a feeling among some Anglos that all Germans were Unionists, and they were subjected to harsh treatment by vigilante groups. Under this pressure, some German civilians fled to Mexico during the war. Some stayed in Mexico, and others returned to Texas later.

The German settlers in Mason County were fairly neutral. These people were not slaveholders; they had come to a new fatherland that promised freedom and opportunity, and they did not want to risk losing these in a war. Nor did they want to see their new country split up into segments. My grandfather, like many others, did not participate in the war. Instead, these men became frontier guardsmen to protect the area against the Indians after the troops were withdrawn from the forts. Some people, not realizing how necessary the guards were, resented the fact that these men were not in the army. One such fellow came to my grandfather's house one day, pulled out his six-shooter and, pointing at the notches on the handle, said, "If you weren't a friend of mine, Ernst, you would be the next."

During World War I there were similar persecutions of the German settlers and their descendants. Although their hearts were not in the war, the German settlers let their sons go to Europe and fight for their new country, just as much as the Anglo settlers did, and they bought Liberty Bonds in greater denominations than most Anglos; still they were hounded because of their German ancestry and language. Finally the Reverend Robert Moerner made a public speech on the steps of the Mason courthouse during one of the bond drives and set the record straight. He ended his address by saying in his German-accented English, "When America is in danger, I will fight like a tiger [he pronounced the word as in German: "teeger"], and so will all the sons of the German settlers." After this episode there were no open confrontations anymore, but petty slurs and prejudiced remarks continued to be heard. Our small community suffered sev-

eral battlefield casualties in France. One of my cousins, Alfred Kothmann, was killed in action, and another cousin, Ernest M. Jordan,
Jr., was seriously wounded.

The fact that Plehweville was one-hundred percent German is
apparent from the family names mentioned above, from the German
spoken at home, and the German-accented English heard in town.
To be sure, Jordan does not sound like a German name, but in our
case it was, and it was pronounced "Yordan." Anyone who has difficulty believing that the name is German should consider the fact that
my immigrant grandfather's full name was Johann Ernst Heinrich
Christian Franz Jordan! That should be German enough to convince
anyone.

My family was an unlikely mixture of different German clans
that came to Texas in the middle of the nineteenth century from
widely separated provinces of central Europe. Certainly few people
besides me and my brothers and sisters ever had a Saxon, a Hessian,
a Silesian, and a Sauerlander as their four grandparents. These immigrants from the four corners of Germany spoke different dialects,
belonged to different churches, and even differed in racial charac-
teristics. In the Hill Country they intermarried and merged their various cultural traditions with each other and ultimately with various
Anglo elements.

My father, Daniel Jordan, was the son of Ernst Jordan, a Lower
Saxon Lutheran from Hannover, and his Evangelical Sauerlander
wife, Lisette Bickenbach. My mother, Emilie Willmann, had a Silesian Catholic father in Anton Willmann and a Lutheran Hessian
mother, Christina Niess. Having such diverse backgrounds, these
couples had to make several important adjustments and compro-
mises. To be sure, they all spoke a form of German, but in different
dialects. Through their marriages and the association with a great
variety of German Texans, their speech leveled off in a mixed or
blended form of High German. Through their contacts with the
Anglo settlers, their language was soon enriched or diluted, as the
case may be, by infusion of English words and anglicisms.

My parents were married in 1883 in an old-fashioned, all-day
German wedding at the new Willmann ranch in Mason County. All
the neighbors and friends and relatives from far and near came, and
they were served two big meals. The first few years of their married

life, my parents lived in the Jordan home with Daniel's family, where their first child, Ida, was born. My mother was amazed by one activity of the first winter here, when the Jordans slaughtered hundreds of mast-fed hogs and cured the bacon, ham, and sausage for sale. The whole family joined in and helped with this commercial hog killing.

My father was a strong, active man with broad shoulders and a full chest. His characteristic posture was with his head upright, looking the world straight in the eye. He always worked hard, tending to his cattle, horses, sheep, and hogs, plowing and cultivating his fields, building and repairing fences, hauling supplies, scraping the sand to dig for water in the creek, butchering and preparing meat for the family, building and repairing barns and sheds, hauling and storing fodder, hay, and grain for his livestock, rounding up, doctoring, branding, and dipping cattle, and working at hundreds of other tasks on the farm and ranch. He believed in the old German saying, *Arbeit macht das Leben süss* ("Work makes life sweet"). He enjoyed a good joke and responded with a hearty laugh. He frequently sang or hummed songs to himself, especially when working on fences or driving one of his vehicles. One of his favorite songs was "Wie lieblich ist's hienieden, wenn Brüder treu gesinnt" ("How lovely it is here below when brothers are true to each other"). When the burdens of life grew heavy and his mind was troubled, he hummed or sang to himself "Wie lange und Schwer wird die Zeit" ("How long and burdensome is time").

During the early years of his married life, he was a *Mädchenvater* ("father of girls"). Five of the six oldest children were girls: Ida, Anna, Dina, Hulda, and Olga (all had names ending in *a*). They had to help him as *Laufjungen* ("errand boys" or general flunky kids) until his first two boys, Daniel (child number five) and Frank (child number seven) grew up and could help. Around the turn of the century, three more babies, Milton, Gilbert, and Emily, were added to round out a family of ten children.

My mother was a small, but strong and active, person. She certainly had the qualifications of a triple-K (*Küche, Kirche, Kinder*: "kitchen, church, children") German *Hausfrau* in the best sense of the words, but it never occurred to anyone to think of her as such. She could be stern when necessary, but she was also loving and kind.

The German children's song that starts with the lines quoted below
describes the relationship between her and her children:

> Ich weiss, die Mama liebt mich,
> Wie sie nur lieben kann;
> Sie sagt's, und o, sie täuscht nicht,
> Sie hat's noch nie getan.
> (*Die Kleine Palme*, 60)

> (I know my mama loves me,
> As loves no other one;
> She says so and deceives not;
> This she has never done.)

Despite the fact that she had a houseful of daughters to help
her, there was always more to do in and around the place than any
group of women could finish. There were the babies to be cared for
and the inevitable housekeeping: setting and clearing the table, washing the dishes and clothes, sweeping, raking, cooking and baking,
sewing, knitting, patching clothes, canning and preserving foods, tending the garden and orchard, milking the cows, feeding the chickens
and hogs, bringing in stove wood, making up beds, making cheese,
sauerkraut, sausage, *Pannas*, and pickles, drying fruit, storing potatoes, and darning socks. My mother stretched the socks over a dried
gourd while she darned them in a sort of basket-weave stitch.

By the time my mother was about fifty years old and had borne
and raised ten children, she began to show symptoms of fatigue.
When my father took her to the family doctor for a medical examination, the physician pronounced her hale and hearty. Then he pulled
a miniature rocking chair out of his desk, showed it to my mother,
and said: "There, that is all the medicine you need. You are good
for another fifty years." He was almost right; my mother lived to be
nearly ninety-seven. Everybody, relatives and friend alike, Germans
and Anglos, all called her *Tante Emilie* ("Aunt Emilie") affection-
ately.

Her favorite song was "Jesus, Heiland meiner Seele" ("Jesus,
Lover of My Soul"). As she grew older and her friends died one
after another, she became more otherworldly, and her favorite song
became:

> Heimatland, Heimatland,
> O wie schön bist du!

Herzinning sehn' ich mich nach dir
Und deiner sel'gen Ruh'.
(*Gesangbuch*, 555)

(Heavenly home, heavenly home,
Oh how fair and blest!
With fervency I yearn for thee
And for thy blissful rest.)

She sang the song often, and the Art Methodist choir sang it in German at her funeral in 1960. In her late years she still had a fabulous memory and could accurately recite German church songs, poems, Bible passages, and prayers for an hour or longer.

After I left home to go to college, and during the many years I was away from them, my parents wrote me hundreds of letters in German, all in the difficult German script. My mother's letters always started with the salutation, "Gottes Segen zum Gruss!" ("God's blessing for a greeting"), and they ended with "Deine, Dich liebende Mama" ("Your own loving Mama").

In 1885 my parents built a small house on 320 acres of land given to them by Grandfather Ernst Jordan. The land lies immediately south of the original Jordan place, and the house, like Daniel's parental home, overlooks the sandy Willow Creek. The building was an expanding and spreading structure. Beginning small, only two rooms wide and a story and a half high, the place grew with the family. Additions in 1891, 1897, 1904, and 1912 resulted in a rambling house with nine rooms and a bath (without toilet) downstairs, two attic rooms, a cellar, and two porches. Most of the house is boxed or frame construction, but stone walls extend all the way across the west side and parts of the north and south sides. Near this building stood the stone smokehouse, and both were enclosed in a yard fence.

There was no special living room in the house. We lived all over the place. Friends and visitors were usually received in the front room, which was my parents' bedroom. My mother kept a trundle bed under her bed and pulled it out at night for some of the children. My father once had an unforgettable experience by the bed. Mother had set traps outside the house for rabbits or rats, but she caught the big old house cat instead. The cat was frightened and furious, ran into the house, and crawled under the bed in the middle of the night. She dragged the trap and chain behind her and screamed like a wildcat. My father tried to get her out and free her, but she clawed and bit and screamed and spit, until the whole family woke up. Finally my father managed to reach the chain and pull her out. Then he threw a quilt over her and freed her foot from the trap.

In this front room there were also several chairs, a table, a marble-top dresser, a foot-powered Singer sewing machine, a chifforobe, and a wood-burning heater. The old family clock stood on a shelf in one corner. This clock made a loud ticking noise that we could hear several rooms away, and the metallic "whang, whang, whang" of the chimes sounded all over the house. Once a week, my father wound the old "whanging" machine. It was very important to keep the clock wound regularly because when it stopped, we had the problem of setting it correctly. There were several methods that could be used to reset it. We could look at the Cardui calendar that hung on the wall near the clock and read the time of sunrise or sunset for any particular day, then set the clock accordingly. Or we could turn to an almanac for the same information. The old Cardui calendars also had weather information and predictions, with little weather flags for every day of the year. Anyone preferring to get the information directly from nature could set his clock by the shadow cast by a hoe handle set up perpendicularly. When the shadow pointed due north, it was 12:00 noon.

Most of the bedrooms did not have heaters. Of course, we had warm quilts, some blankets, and feather beds, but even so, it was a chilly shock to crawl into bed in extremely cold weather. Sometimes my mother heated stones or bricks, wrapped them in towels, and put them in our beds to prewarm them. In summer we opened all the doors and windows wide and let the Texas Hill Country breeze keep us cool.

The most interesting room in the house was the parlor. It was built just in time for the girls to have a place to entertain their friends. It was a sort of country sitting room but was used only for special events like midweek prayer meetings, for sleeping or entertaining very special guests, for play parties, singing, courting, weddings, honeymoons, viewing stereoscopic pictures, playing the organ, and looking at family albums. When the room was not in use, the door, the six windows, and their outside wooden shutters were tightly closed. Obviously shutters were made to be shut.

There were several family albums in the parlor. They contained mostly wedding pictures of the family and of all our friends and relatives. Bound in red or blue velvet, the albums had metallic decorations and curlicues on the outside and a metal latch. In the back covers were Swiss or German music boxes that played cheerful melodies when the albums were opened.

On the walls were a few Biblical pictures like those by the German painter Schnorr von Karolsfeld and some enlargements of family photographs, and on the floor was an "art-square" rug. Everywhere was the typical nineteenth century bric-a-brac: seashells, dried or artificial flowers placed in standing glass cases, peacock feathers in vases, some crocheted doilies, white, lacy tablecloths, several Victorian, coal-oil-burning china lamps with painted roses and chrysanthemums, one silver lamp with a white china shade, and finally the gigantic family Bible with thick, embossed covers.

This Bible was actually used only on special occasions, perhaps by the preacher during the home prayer meetings, but the Bible also served as the record book for the births, marriages, and deaths in the family. For some reason, all the double names of our family are recorded with the middle name first, so my name appears as Johann Gilbert Jordan.

The prize possession in our parlor was the pump organ. With its bold front, it was as tall as the horse that my father traded for it. Above the keyboard there was the usual console, with holders for sheet music and songbooks, some shelves for bric-a-brac and books, a mirror, and little railings. My sisters had music lessons from Otto von Plehwe, who was a schoolmaster from Berlin. My sisters played mostly church songs because our family, like the whole community of Plehweville, was church-centered. Occasionally the family stood around in a semicircle and sang in German "Er führet mich" ("He Leadeth Me") and "Welch ein treuer Freund ist Jesus" ("What a Friend We Have in Jesus") or in English "When the Roll Is Called up Yonder, I'll Be There," "Blessed Assurance," and "Bringing in the Sheaves" or many of the other English and German church and Sunday school songs we loved. We also sang "The Church in the Wildwood." I don't know why we liked this song, since our church was in neither a wildwood nor a dale. It stood on a high spot by the public road between Mason and Llano, and it looked down on the Willow Creek. We probably liked the rhythmic "come, come, come, come, come" line with its crescendo of bass notes. If we had used a little imagination, we might have sung: "Oh, come, come, come, come, come to the church by the Willow; oh, come to the church on the hill."

To round out our musical activity, my brother Milton played a German Hohner mouth harmonica, some of my sisters plucked our imported zither, and my little sister Emily and I played the music boxes in the back of the picture albums. Later on, during the second decade of the century, we also had an old-fashioned phonograph with a big morning-glory horn and cylindrical records, but the music it produced was thin and tinny. It belonged to my father's cousin Fred Bickenbach, who lived with us and worked for us as a farmhand. My father wasn't about to spend his good money for "canned" music from a gramophone that sounded no better than a telephone.

The parlor was a good place for courting, but in winter it sometimes got too cold, and in summer, too hot. In the early days, pranksters presented a very real problem. As soon as a boyfriend became a regular caller, his acquaintances plotted mischief. If the fellow made his calls on horseback, he might discover that his saddle was missing or reversed on the horse or that the stirrups were tied hard and fast across the seat. If he came in a buggy, he was likely to find one of the tall, rear wheels in front and one of the little, front wheels in the rear. Or the reins might be crisscrossed, so that the horse turned left when the driver pulled the right rein. If a boy walked to a neighbor's place to call on a girl, he would likely fall flat on his face when he returned home in the dark and tripped over a rope or wire stretched across the road or path. One trick that worked well on buggy riders and horsemen alike was the wired gate. Undoing and opening the gate might take hours, perhaps until daylight the next morning. The car courters of the second and third decades of the century fared no better, what with deflated tires, crossed wires on the spark plugs, or a drained radiator or gasoline tank.

When my oldest sister, Ida, married John Schuessler in 1905, my parents went all out to give an old-fashioned, all-day German wedding, like their own twenty-three years earlier. All the relatives and friends of the two families, about one-fourth of Mason County plus Castell in Llano County, came to the affair. The German word for "wedding" is *Hochzeit*, a "high time," and that is what it was, a high and festive time. A big shed covered with wagon sheets was built across the backyard, and there were long, board tables and benches. The proverbial fatted calf was killed and served up at the big feast.

The wedding itself was indoors in the newly built parlor. The preacher, my uncle the Reverend Heinrich Jordan, read the usual southern Methodist ritual, in which the bride promised to obey, serve, love, honor, and keep her life's companion. Although the northern branch of the church had deleted the word *obey* from its discipline, the southern church continued to use it. The phrasing in German was, "Willst du ihm gehorsam sein?" (literally, "Wilt thou be obedient to him?"). The minister also preached a long German sermon. A morning ceremony left the rest of the day free for eating, talking, and celebrating. In those early days, the newlywed couple did not run off on a honeymoon. There was no place to run to, and our parlor was a good substitute.

This wedding must have taken the steam out of my father. Although he had a respite of nine years before the next wedding, there never was another big blast. After all, there were five other daughters to think about. Three of the others, Anna, Hulda, and Olga, also had home weddings, but much smaller. These home weddings continued to be favored until the 1920's, when church weddings became more popular.

In summer our L-shaped front porch or gallery served as a living or sitting room, and that wasn't a bad idea. Here we had various wooden benches and chairs. On one wall was our thermometer. When the mercury rose to the 90's and 100's, we used the porch for taking naps at noon and for sleeping at night. This porch was also the place where we let peddlers like Mr. Kahn, the traveling clothes dealer, and Mr. Schweers, the Watkins man, spread out their wares for inspection and sales. I always liked to see Mr. Schweers come and unpack his fragrant soap. It smelled so much better than our home-made lye soap. To show that he and his goods were welcome, we would invite him to our backyard to eat watermelons. He ate them voraciously, sometimes seeds and all. He weighed 250 to 300 pounds and had an enormous capacity for food.

The front porch also served as a sleeping area when our relatives on my mother's side, with their large families, came from Gillespie, Bexar, Comal, and Mason counties to visit and spend several weeks with us in the summer. The old folk and the girls took over the bedrooms, hall, and parlor; we boys slept on pallets all over the porch. Even so, I do not see how several large families found a place to sleep and eat. One thing is sure: these hungry relatives filled up on good, solid country food, and they left many empty spaces in our ham, bacon, and sausage larders and in our general food supply. Fortunately, the garden and orchard were in their prime, and the boys ate peaches in excessive quantities, like the Okies in John Steinbeck's novel *The Grapes of Wrath*; they suffered the same consequences as the Okies did in California.

We had a cool, so-called hall that separated the parlor from the rest of the house. It was built like a breezeway, but it was completely closed in, with doors leading to the porch on the south, to the outdoors on the north, to the parlor on the east, and to a bedroom on the west. At times we had a bed there, and then the hall served as a spare bedroom. At Christmastime the bed was taken down, and the hall became our Christmas room, where we had our tree and gifts. The room was almost as well isolated as the parlor next to it. My parents and older sisters could decorate the Christmas tree undisturbed and put the presents under the tree unobserved. Then they would tell the children that Santa Claus had come.

The hall was also our funeral parlor. When I was ten years old, in 1913, we had two deaths in the family within less than one week. My sister Dina died in Austin on November 3, and my grandmother Christina Willmann died in our home on November 7. In both cases the night watch or wake was kept and the home funeral services were held in the hall. These two deaths, coming so close together, were almost more than we could bear, especially my mother. I remember all too well how she wept over Dina, kissed her on her cold forehead, and cried in anguish, "O, mein armes kind" ("Oh, my poor child"), as the body lay in the open coffin in the hall.

Grandmother had been living with us for several years. The last remodeling and enlargement of our house was done to add a room for her. She had a disjointed or broken hip and walked with much difficulty with the aid of crutches. Her death was almost a relief, but, coming only a few days after Dina's funeral, it added greatly to my mother's sorrow. Dina had been away from home for several years, first as a student at Southwestern University in Georgetown, then as a missionary of the German Mission Conference of the southern Methodist Church. She was stationed at the San Marcos Street German Methodist Church in San Antonio before her death. She wrote letters in which she told of her health problems and worries and her premonitions of death and dreams of dying. My parents took her to Austin for an operation, and there she died of pneumonia after weeks of suffering. My father brought her body home, by train as far as Llano and then by hack the rest of the way. Because of heavy rains, high water, and detours, the drive from Llano to our home took several days. My mother cried: "Why didn't God let me or Grandmother die in her place? We are old, and Dina was still so young." She was twenty-two.

My sisters Dina and Anna were the first members of our family to go to college. Later a few of the others also went, and two of us completed the course at Southwestern University. In those earlier days few rural people felt the need for higher education, certainly not for girls, and I am still puzzled why my parents let some of the older girls go to college. In general, though, the German Methodists seem to have stressed higher education more and earlier than other groups in our part of the country.

We had two large attic rooms in our house, and for many years these rooms served as sleeping quarters for the hired man or men. We also used one of these rooms for ripening late fall tomatoes and for mellowing pears. There was also attic storage space and a play area for the children.

Under the north section of the house was a cellar. Sandstone steps led down to the cool room with its thick masonry walls. This was our storeroom for Irish potatoes and onions, great quantities of bacon, ham, and sausage hanging from overhead beams, crocks of sauerkraut and pickles, jars of canned food, and a keg of sweet wine.

As in all rural homes, the kitchen and dining room were the scene of endless activity. On the south side of the kitchen was a little porch with trumpet vines growing on the sunny side. The porch served as a sheltered entrance to the kitchen and dining room, but its main function was that of an outdoor washing area. Here we had a long wash bench with three or four washbasins, soap dishes, and a faucet that flowed fresh water from our new waterworks. On the wall near the bench were a comb holder, a mirror, and nails for hanging towels and hats. Here the menfolk washed their hands and faces, then poured the used water into the yard or on the trumpet-vine roots before entering the house.

If the main residence was a spreading house, then our entire farmstead was a creeping layout. As it grew larger, it soon spread out in all directions beyond the original fenced yard. To the southwest and west stood farm and ranch buildings: a crib and barn, with stables built of logs and lumber, a pen for the horses, a sheepfold bounded on the north by a stone fence, and the old log smokehouse. The smokehouse was enlarged by attaching a lean-to on the back to shelter farm machinery and some of our vehicles, and two side sheds were added, one for the hack or surrey and the other for the sweet-potato sandbox and chicken feed. Our log cribs were rustic and primitive. They were built of rough post-oak logs joined at the corners by a common saddle notch. The cracks between the logs were left slightly open to ventilate the corn.

Nearby stood a chicken house, a chicken coop, a second sheep-fold, a buggy shed, and a little two-holer outhouse for the women. We called this outdoor toilet a *Häuschen* ("little house"). Also to the west was the big woodpile. We burned dry post-oak wood in our cook stove and mesquite wood in our heaters. Near the woodpile were the beehives. When we kept at a respectable distance from the bees, they did not bother us. There was also a large, horse-drawn corn crusher, in which we could grind corn, cobs and all, for our horses and other livestock. We really played a dirty trick on the horses when we ground the cobs with the grains of corn. The horses didn't need all this roughage, considering how much hay, corn-top fodder, and grass they ate anyway.

To the north was the new, two-story, red-frame barn and stable. It had a drive-through in the center, and a number of horse stalls, a saddle and harness room, a grain bin, a cattle-feed room, two large hay and fodder lofts, and in the front a fenced horse yard. Nearby were additional pens with a cypress trough that extended through the fence. The main cowpens were across the road to the east, partly in front of our house, as were the pigpen and shed. Inside the cowpens was an old log crib in which we kept feed for the milch cows and hogs, and behind the crib were small pens and the chute for branding and doctoring cattle. At first these pens were enclosed with zigzag or snake-rail fences, but these were later replaced by the better post-and-rail construction. On the north, some stone fences served as windbreaks in winter. Pens enclosed with rail fences offered a great advantage when a wild steer or hog came after us. In an emergency we could climb rails easier than stone, picket, or wire fences.

Near our house was an old-fashioned dug well from which we drew our household water. It was important to have a good well close to the house. Sometimes it was difficult to dig a well at a convenient location, so well digging became a neighborhood project, something like the old logrollings when everybody helped build a neighbor's house. There were a few specialists among the well diggers, like Clemens Mueller, and they supervised the digging, but much of the labor was performed by the family members themselves and their friends and neighbors.

The digger was let down and pulled out by a homemade windlass, and the dirt and rocks were pulled out in big buckets in the same way. When solid-rock strata had to be penetrated, the diggers set off blasts of dynamite. This was dangerous because of the difficulty in igniting the fuses and getting out before the explosion. For this reason live coals were poured into the well to ignite the dynamite fuses. After the blast, noxious fumes were a problem, and the well had to be aired out.

After the digging was completed, a stonemason lined the well, or at least the upper part of it, with a round wall. Then he built the stone curbing about three feet above the ground. On top he mounted a large one-piece flat stone, with a two- to three-foot hole chiseled in the center, and fastened it to the wall with lime mortar. Then he installed the metal frame for the pulley wheel. To mount it firmly, he drilled holes into the stone and inserted the bottom ends of the frame. To hold the frame securely, he poured in melted sulphur to cement the frame to the stone. Finally the men installed the pulley wheel, the rope or chain, and the buckets. Now they could draw cool well water and drink a toast with pure *Gänsewein* ("goose wine") from the new well.

Mason County and the Texas German Belt had many such

wells. Some still exist, and a few are still in use. The best one I know in Mason County is at the old Wilhelm Koock place in Koocksville, near Mason, but we and some of our neighbors, the Otto Donops and the Hermann Standkes, also had stone wells. In fact, we had two of these dug wells, from which we drew out by hand all the water for home use and for our farm animals. The second well was near the little creek and it had a wooden trough by its side for watering livestock.

When Sister Olga and Brother Frank were small children, they played near this old trough. Olga remembered her Sunday-school lesson about Jesus walking on the water and took it to heart. One day she climbed up on the edge of the water trough and proclaimed, "Now I will walk on the water, just like Jesus." Before Frank realized fully what was happening, she slipped off the edge of the trough, fell into the water, and went down like a sinker. Frank was scared to death and ran to the house, panting, "Olga, Wasser! Olga, Wasser! Olga, Wasser!" Because Frank was so excited and bewildered, everybody thought Olga had fallen into the well, and they all dashed out to rescue her. About that time Olga came waddling up the bank of the creek, her heavy winter clothes dripping wet.

About 1908 Christian Vater drilled a new well for us with a small drilling rig and put up an Aermotor windmill, which is still functioning. He also installed waterworks and a large metal tank. This new well furnished abundant water for livestock, for home use, for the irrigation of flowers in the yard, and for vegetables in the garden. My mother and her daughters loved their petunias, periwinkles, violets, zinnias, roses, iris, phlox, red amaryllis, portulaca, pansies (Johnny-jump-ups), plumbago, the rosemary bush, and the honeysuckle and trumpet vines. They also had a stair-step shelf on the front porch for potted geraniums, ferns, and plumbago plants. Now they had plenty of fresh water.

During periods of calm, when the wind did not turn the windmill enough, we had to watch the water gauge on the tank carefully and not let the water level go down too low. The float on the inside of the tank went down with the falling water level, and the outside weight went up. The higher the gauge, the lower the water level. When the water level got too low, the plants were sacrificed so that the people and animals would have enough water.

I was still a little kid when our new well was drilled and the windmill erected. I would have given almost anything to watch all this activity at close range, but I was sick at the time and could see only a little of the raising of the windmill through a window by my bed. Later, when I was a teenager, I became the grease monkey and climbed to the top of the windmill tower with my little oil can. This was a dizzy business, and I was always afraid I would fall, especially when the wind was blowing. And it seems that it always blew when I got to the top. But no matter how much I dreaded to climb the derrick to oil the motor, I was always fond of windmills and enjoyed hearing the roaring of the big wheel and the "klank, klonk" sound of the pump gears.

Rural families were self-sufficient in the nineteenth and early twentieth centuries. We soled our own shoes with our cobbler's tools and repaired broken seams and cracks. In summer the smaller children went barefoot most of the time, and that saved the shoes, but grassburs presented a real problem. We called a grassbur a *Wehkuss* in German, a "kiss of woe" or an "ouch kiss." We also serviced other leather goods like saddles and harnesses. We greased our own vehicles: the wagons, buggies, hacks, surreys, and gigs. My brother-in-law, Edwin Donop, Hulda's husband, used to say, "Wer gut schmiert, der gut fährt" ("He who greases well, drives well"). We believed this dictum and smeared on lots of axle grease. And when we got our first car, we continued to grease well. As might be expected, the cup grease oozed out of the front wheel bearings and dripped all over the sides of the wheels and tires.

We relined the brake shoes on our vehicles about once each year by nailing on the soles of old, worn-out shoes. No wonder the braking blocks were called brake shoes. When the metal tires on our wagon and buggy wheels became loose in summer, we soaked the wooden rims in boiling linseed oil. My father had a big half-moon-shaped pan about a yard long and as wide as the widest rims. He jacked up one wheel at a time, placed the pan under the wheel, and poured in some boiling linseed oil. We turned the wheel slowly until it got thoroughly soaked in oil. This remedy was as effective for loose wagon wheels as castor oil was for a constipated ranchhand. The only difference was that one tightened and the other loosened. All the farmers and ranchmen greased their own vehicles. They removed the big nut on the axle, pulled the wheel off partway, smeared on some axle grease, and fastened the wheel back on again. We repaired our own fences, gates, and buildings, and we painted our house from time to time. If anybody had asked us when we did all this repair work, we could have answered truthfully, "Always."

Shoeing horses (we called it *die Pferde beschlagen*) was a periodic chore. The English word *horseshoes* is really not very descriptive; in German we called them *Hufeisen* ("hoof irons"). Our horses were hard on shoes because they traveled much on coarse sand, gravel, and rocks. Most horses were patient and let us trim their hooves, rasp the bottom flat for an exact fitting, nail on the iron shoe, and rasp the whole hoof smooth, but some horses were natural rebels. It was a tricky business to hammer the flat, sharp nails into the hooves in such a way that the points of the nails emerged at the right place, then to snip off the nails and clinch them. If the nail was driven in too deep, the horse jerked and became lame. Or if the nails were not driven in deep enough, the horseshoe came off before it wore out. There was always a dangerous moment when the nail was driven in and the sharp point emerged. If the horse jerked or jumped, the shoer might get slashed.

There were also regular cleaning jobs to do in the horse yards, the cowpens, the pigpens, the sheepfolds, and the henhouse. This cleanup gave us an abundant supply of manure, and we hauled it as fertilizer to the fields, garden, orchard, and flower beds, just as farmers in Germany do.

Every Saturday we children had to shuck corn by hand and then shell it by the bushel with the corn sheller, which had a crank and a big flywheel. One of us turned the crank until the flywheel hummed, and a second one fed the shucked ears of corn in as fast as the sheller swallowed them. The cobs came out on one side of the big wooden case and the shelled corn poured out underneath. We saved some of the cobs to be used by the men later, in place of the Sears-Roebuck catalogues used by the women. Then we carried the shelled corn and other cow feed to several cribs and bins so that it was ready and handy for morning and evening feeding.

Before the children went to school in the morning and after they returned in the afternoon, they had to help with the regular chores. They fed the milch cows, horses, hogs, chickens, dogs, and cats; they milked the cows, rounded up and counted the sheep in the afternoons, gathered the eggs, chopped and brought in stove wood. The girls worked in the kitchen and garden; they helped prepare supper and breakfast; they set and cleared the table, washed the dishes, swept and cleaned the house, and raked the yard from time to time.

Sharpening tools was a regular activity at our place. We had a large, round grindstone mounted on two mesquite posts under a live-oak tree. Here we sharpened our axes, hatchets, hoes, knives, sickles, and scythes. While one of the adults held the tool to the grindstone, one of us kids turned the crank and poured water on the stone.

We made our own laundry soap out of lard and lye. The mixture had to be boiled until it got stringy, poured into long wooden forms, and then, after it got firm, cut into squares. It turned a dark brown-and-tan color. In my days we had hand-operated washing machines and wringers, but we also used scrub boards and rubbed the work clothes until they were threadbare. Boiling, scrubbing, rinsing, bluing, wringing, hanging out, and ironing clothes was a major activity once each week.

Ironing great piles of work and dress clothes must have been the women's worst and hardest work. The old flatirons had to be heated on the hot cookstove, and in summer the stove heated up the whole work area and made the ironing almost unbearable. This work was certainly never shared by the men, and the little boys couldn't help either. So the women struggled with white, starched dresses with miles of lacy trim, and with hard, stiff collars and cuffs.

Quilting was a more pleasant activity than washing and ironing for most rural women because it was a sort of community activity. Occasional quilting parties brought the women together and incidentally provided quilts for the family and for the hope chests of the girls. Much work had to be done before the quilting party started. The cotton was carded, the patchwork pieced together by hand, and the two layers of material and the carded cotton stretched on a frame. At this point the party started, and the women stitched the layers together.

My mother cut my father's and her sons' hair until her boys were grown. Later, Brothers Dan and Frank took over the barber work. When I was a little boy, my older sisters were fond of my curly hair and tried to keep my mother from cutting it. They told me that my poor curls would bleed if Mama cut them off. So when my mother decided it was time to make me look more like a boy by giving me a haircut, I yelled and screamed bloody murder. We had quite a hassle, but she finally whacked off my girlish curls. I had earlier shed my pretty red dress, the kind worn in those days by all children, including little boys.

About once each week all the coal-oil lamps and lanterns had to be filled, the wicks cut straight on top, and the lamp chimneys cleaned. The ashes were shoveled from the heaters and from the cookstove into big buckets and then carried out and emptied on our ash heap behind the farm buildings.

But not all was work at our home; we played various simple games and we had both store-bought and homemade toys. Our favorite indoor games were single-spinner dominoes and *Mühle* ("mill"). The board for the latter game was homemade, and we used grains of corn or buttons of different colors for our movable pieces. No cards were ever permitted in our home, but we did occasionally play forty-two with our dominoes. Outside we played baseball, mostly pitch and catch, footracing, hide and seek, horseshoe pitching, and other simple games. By the time I came along, we had little red wagons, tricycles, and homemade cars. The little car I made was crude, but it could be guided by a steering wheel, and it had candle-burning lamps made of tin cans. The girls naturally had their dolls with painted china heads and hands and sawdust-stuffed bodies. They also had a cast-iron stove, a small replica of our big kitchen range. We could build a fire in the fire box when we played outside. We did not do this often, though, because we were taught that kids who play with fire wet their beds.

Country children often made up their own games. We had our corncob cows, peach-seed turkeys, stick horses, and imaginary ranches. We rounded up our herds of cattle, roped, branded, and sold them, and we drove them from pasture to pasture.

As we grew older, we entered into more realistic activities. Roping required much practice. At first, before we learned to lasso calves, we tried to rope stumps and fence posts or dogs, chickens, and turkeys. Chickens and turkeys are hard to rope because their heads are small and they jump or run away when you throw a rope at them.

Brother Dan and Cousin Ernest Jordan found a solution to this problem. At their Grandmother Jordan's house they discovered a setting hen, roped her, and pulled her off the nest. Then they proudly carried the big cache of eggs into the house in their hands and pockets, only to discover that the half-hatched eggs were broken, oozing out of their pants, and running down their legs. By that time their pockets contained nothing but embryonic chicks and egg shells.

Our reading matter, in addition to schoolbooks, was largely church and Sunday-school literature, the Bible, a few German and English newspapers, some fairy tales, almanacs, and mail-order catalogues. Several books on special events like the sinking of the *Titanic* were available, but very little in the field of literature. There was *Der Missionsfreund* ("The Mission Friend"), *Der Christliche Apologete* ("The Christian Apologist"), *Der Texas Stern* ("The Texas Star"), the *Mason County News*, and *Farm and Ranch*. We began to get a daily paper, the *Austin American*, during World War I. I still remember its comic strips, for example, "Mutt and Jeff," "Bringing up Father" (Maggie and Jiggs), and "The Katzenjammer Kids."

We did not have to rely altogether on books and newspapers for our information and entertainment because my father was a good storyteller. He told many Indian tales, for instance, the account of the kidnapping of Wilhelm Hoerster, which Father witnessed in broad daylight. Wilhelm was guarding the family's horses when a band of Indians appeared, roped him with a rawhide rope, tied him on a horse, and carried him away with the horses they stole. Fortunately, he was able to return home about a year later when he was ransomed. There were also the stories about the kidnapping of Adolph Korn, Wilhelm Lehmann, and Wilhelm's brother Hermann. And Father told us about the time when his father was sitting on the porch late at night, and an Indian sneaked into the yard and tried to steal the horse that was tied to a tree near the house. Ernst shouted a loud "hello," and the intruder left quickly. Then there was a dreadful story about the torture and slaying of Heinrich and Johanne Kensing. The Indian raids and killings frightened both children and adults. To relieve the tension caused by telling about so many serious happenings, Father added a humorous Indian story about himself and his younger brother Ernst.

As little boys, so his story went, Daniel and Ernst were imitating their father by making long "trips" in ox wagons hauling supplies from San Antonio and Indianola. They made their own yokes of toy oxen out of corncobs, and took "trips" up and down the Willow Creek. About one-half mile down the creek was their Indianola, and their intermediate points were Austin and San Antonio. One day while they were on one of these trips, an Indian appeared. In fright the boys deserted their oxen and wagons, ran toward home, and jumped over a rail fence, not looking back for fear that they might see the Indian ready to seize them. They arrived home safely and threw themselves into their mother's arms. Never again would they venture so far into Indian territory. Years later, when they had grown past the age of corncob oxen, they learned that the "Indian" they had seen was none other than their own sister Sophie who had been sent to frighten them lest they stray too far from home.

Father also told true stories about the terrible times of the Mason County "Hoodoo War" (Who do it—so called since mystery surrounded several of the killings) in the 1870's, during which his brother-in-law Daniel Hoerster was killed and his own brother Peter was wounded when they were ambushed by a gang of outlaws and cattle rustlers. Hoerster was county brands inspector and he had incriminating evidence against the cattle thieves. As Hoerster and Jordan rode into town, some outlaws who lay in wait behind a building attacked them. When the men opened fire, Daniel Hoerster fell dead from his horse in the first volley of shots, but Peter Jordan and Heinrich Pluenneke drove the outlaws away with rifle fire.

There were also a number of humorous anecdotes in Father's repertory. Three Klein brothers, according to his story, came to Texas from Germany. The first one kept his name unchanged and spelled it as it is spelled in German: "Klein." The second one anglicized the spelling to "Cline," and the third translated his name to "Small." Years later when a large inheritance came from Germany, Mr. Klein got all of it, and Mr. Cline and Mr. Small were left out completely. Father's moral was: do not renounce your heritage.

His story about the rake always amused me, especially in retrospect after I went to college. A German-Texas farmer, so the story goes, sent his son to college to learn a thing or two. Sonny Boy got so carried away by all the learning and culture he absorbed in his higher education that he put on airs and pretended to forget his German and everything about his earlier life on the farm. When he came back to visit the old folks at home, he made it a point to ask his father about all the "strange" things and animals he saw. "What's that thing over there, Papa?" "That's a plow, Son." "What's that animal in the pen, Papa?" "That's a cow, Son." The question and answer ceremony continued for some time until they came to a fence, against which a hand rake was leaning with its teeth turned up. Again he asked his father, "What is this thing leaning against the fence?" Before the father could answer, the boy stepped on the teeth of the rake unintentionally, and the handle of the rake hit him right smack in his face. The powerful blow brought back his failing memory, even his childhood German, and he said without hesitation, "Verdammter Rechen!" ("damned rake").

Another favorite story was about the little fellow who always got pushed back by others. Instead of complaining, he just stood back and said philosophically, "Wer weiss, wofür das gut ist!" ("Who knows what good may come of that"). On one occasion he and a group of men were about to go down in an elevator shaft to inspect a deep mine. As usual our little man was pushed back and did not get into the elevator. During the descent, the cable broke, and all the men in the elevator were killed. *Wer weiss, wofür das gut ist!*

My father often sang a little German song to us children. It is similar to "Old McDonald Had a Farm," and it builds up a long repetitive sequence about a meadow, a tree, a limb, a branch, a twig, a nest, an egg, a yolk, and a bird. The song begins with the refrain, "Droben auf grüner Heide steht ein Birnbaum, trägt Laub" ("Yonder on the green meadow stands a pear tree bearing leaves"). Then it proceeds with questions and answers like, "Was ist denn an dem Baum?—Ein wunderschöner Ast" ("What is on the tree?—A very beautiful limb"), followed each time by a repetition of all the previously named items in reverse order, plus the refrain. The final stanza then goes as follows:

Vogel im Dotter, Dotter im Ei, Ei im Nest, Nest am Quast, Quast am Ast, Ast am Baum, Baum in der Erd: Droben auf grüner Heide steht ein Birnbaum, trägt Laub ("Bird in yolk, yolk in egg, egg in nest, nest on twig, twig on limb, limb on tree, tree in ground: Yonder on the green meadow stands a pear tree bearing leaves").

Telephones, too, eventually provided much entertainment for the isolated rural families. When the farm and ranch women found some spare time, they visited by phone, and some of them enjoyed these visits so much that they indulged themselves even when they had no time to spare. You could call a friend or let the friend call you, or you could take up the receiver on the party line and listen in on your neighbors' conversations. Each rural party line had from five to fifteen phones. To call someone on your line, you turned the little crank on the right side of the wall-mounted telephone box. Each family had its own "ring," like ours: one long and one short. Other rings were any of these combinations: long, short, long; short, long; short, long, short; short, short, long; and so on in many sequences. We listed these rings by drawing the proper long and short lines by the names of our friends and hung the listing on the wall by the side of the phone box. We called our friends directly, with no operator assistance. This was a far cry from Grandfather Ernst Jordan's warning system, a rifle shot.

To call people on other lines we rang one long ring to call the central office in Mason. When "central" answered, we gave her the name of the person, the residence, or the business firm we wanted, and the operator (we always called the operator "central") made the connection and rang the desired signal on the other line. When we couldn't hear a person on the other end of the line well enough, we shook and rattled our receiver hook. Sometimes this helped, but usually it did not. If not, we asked the telephone eavesdroppers to hang up their receivers. Few of them responded unless it was an emergency, and, even when they did, the connections remained bad.

The Martins from Llano installed our first phones around 1910, and they serviced the main lines. The local or rural lines were usually built and kept in repair by the farmers and ranchmen themselves. Later a telephone book was printed. To make it possible to list "rings" in the book, a system of numerical listings was devised. Every signal then had to start with a long ring. Thus the first digit indicated the number of long rings, and the second digit showed the number of short rings to follow. By this system then, one long and one short ring were listed as 11, one long and two short appeared as 12, two longs and one short were 21, and so on through the whole set of rings.

We might say, then, that Plehweville was a typical, spread-out German settlement on the Willow Creek in Mason County, not unlike many others throughout the Hill Country and other areas of west-central Texas. The people raised large families and transmitted their German names to the present time; they built their scattered houses on large tracts of recently acquired land; they lived and labored in their homes and on their ranches in a characteristic rural style, strongly flavored by German traditions; and they built their rural schools and churches in central locations, where these institutions became the focal point of their community life. Most German communities were somewhat isolated, but there was some communication between the various settlements, largely through the churches.

3

Bless, Our Father,
This Our Food

THE food German-Texans ate showed both German and Anglo influences, as did other cultural elements of our lives. Following German tradition, these settlers prepared more sausage and cheese and had a greater variety of them than the Anglo Texans. They continued to cultivate the vegetables they had known in Germany, and they made sauerkraut just as they had done in their former homeland. On the other hand, they supplemented their diet by adding American foods like ham and eggs, beef steak, roast turkey, sweet potatoes, corn, squash, tomatoes, and melons, without sacrificing their traditional German fare.

In my parental home, we ate three regular meals each day, as surely as the sun rose and set. We called the meals *Frühstück* ("breakfast"), *Mittagessen* ("dinner at noon"), and *Abendessen* ("supper"). The whole family ate together at the big dining table. We sat quietly on the long bench and the chairs around the table, folded our hands, and bowed our heads. My father usually spoke the memorized German blessing:

> Segne, Vater, diese Speise,
> Uns zur Kraft und Dir sum Preise.
>
> (Bless, Our Father, this our food,
> For Thy glory and our good.)

My mother preferred the following prayer:

> Komm, Herr Jesu, sei unser Gast,
> Und segne, was Du uns bescheret hast.
>
> (Come, Lord Jesus, be our guest
> And let the food you gave be blessed.)

I remember a charming verse about table prayers that my sister-in-law Dina Treibs Jordan once recited to me:

> Wer ohne Gebet zu Tische geht,
> Wer ohne Gebet vom Tische aufsteht,
> Der ist dem Ochs und Esel gleich,
> Und kommt auch nicht ins Himmelreich.

> (Who without prayer at the table will sup,
> Who without prayer from the table gets up,
> He's like an ox and a donkey, dumb,
> And will never to the kingdom of heaven come.)

The little verse may sound funny to some readers now, but it was, no doubt, composed with serious intent.

After the prayers were spoken, the family members turned their plates right side up in unison, the food was passed around, and everybody helped himself. Passing the food and people helping themselves remind me of an old bachelor named Peter Flint. At one time he attended a big wedding dinner near Castell. When the bowl of *Schmierkäs'* was passed to him, he was so hungry for good, creamy, homemade cheese that he emptied half of it on his plate. Then he said to his friend Peter Lange, "Peter, willst du Käs', wenn nicht, so nehm' ich ihn alle" ("Peter, do you want cheese? If not, I'll take it all"), and he ladled out the rest of the cheese on his plate before Lange could answer.

Homemade bread was served regularly, and you might say that every meal started with a blessing and bread. My mother and my older sisters baked wheat bread on Mondays, Wednesdays, Fridays, and Saturdays. This was a regular item in our diet, and we ate it with everything. When we prayed "Give us this day our daily bread," we could use the word *bread* both literally, meaning wheat bread, and figuratively, meaning food. And the Lord and my mother saw to it that we had our bread, not only daily, but three times daily. We children were always discouraged from eating between meals, but if we happened to be in the kitchen when fresh-baked bread with thick, brown crusts was pulled from the oven, exceptions to the rule were made. We could eat a slice of this bread with butter and honey or preserves. When the bread had holes in it, we were told that the baker had crawled through. *Hefekuchen* was a sweet bread, but we never called it a bread. Mama put only a little sugar in the dough because the sugar might prevent the proper rising. Instead, she made a topping of butter, sugar, and cinnamon, and she put this *Streusel* on the cake at two-inch intervals. This made the top of the square cake look tufted, like a mattress.

In my family nobody ever said "pass the biscuits, please" because there seldom were any. I found out how good biscuits can be only after I married an East Texas girl, Vera Belle Tiller of Elysian Fields. Her mother, Mrs. Pearl Weeks Tiller, baked biscuits several times a day, and these biscuits melted in your mouth when spread with homemade butter and fig or pear preserves. East Texans also eat a lot of corn bread and sometimes corn pone. We, too, had corn bread occasionally, but not as often as the people in East Texas.

There was plenty of food at all times, but none was ever wasted. Our mother taught us that it is sinful to waste food, and we believed it. Everybody could take on his plate as much as he wanted, but he was expected to eat what he took. We learned to gauge our appetites and capacities.

Our breakfast was somewhat anglicized, inasmuch as we ate bacon and eggs or ham and eggs in true Texas style. We also had cooked cereals like oatmeal, called *Hafergrütze* in German, and cream of wheat. I remember very well the cream-of-wheat carton with the picture of a black chef wearing a tall hat and bringing in a carton of cream of wheat. On this picture was another, much smaller picture of the same chef, again bringing in a carton of cream of wheat; and on this very small carton the same black chef with a carton of cream of wheat could again be seen. Seeing these pictures within ever smaller pictures prompted my first reflections on infinity. Theoretically, this thing could go on forever, just like time and space. It was more than I could grasp.

We also had two or three kinds of food for breakfast that were characteristic of Texas-German culture: *Kochwurst*, a cooked and fried pork-and-liver sausage; *Pannas*, a fried cornmeal by-product of cooking the *Kochwurst*; and *Schmierkäs'*, a homemade cottage cheese, which we also ate for supper. At noon we had the main meal of the day. Usually there was some kind of meat: roast beef, steak, fried ribs, sausage, cured ham—either fried or baked—sometimes bacon, and, often enough, fried chicken. Sometimes mutton or lamb was served and, in the fall, roast pork. As might be expected, there were all kinds of vegetables (*Gemüse*) from our garden: green beans in cream sauce or in vinegar sauce with onions, English peas, okra, fresh or cooked tomatoes, pickled beets, turnips in a white sauce, cooked greens, dry beans, boiled or mashed potatoes, fresh radishes, leaf lettuce in a sugar-vinegar sauce, cucumbers in a cream sauce, cooked cabbage, and onions. From the field came corn, which we always called "roasting ears," never "corn on the cob," cushaws, pumpkins, and field peas. We ate more cabbage than people do now: cooked cabbage, raw cole slaw in a sweet creamy sauce, and home-made sauerkraut that we kept in large crocks in our cellar.

Our evening meal was always called "supper" in English and *Abendessen* in German. In the busy summer season supper often came late. If there was any food left over from the noon meal, it was warmed over and appeared again on the supper table. To supplement the leftovers or to take their place if there were only few or none, we sometimes had pancakes, scrambled eggs, *Schmierkäs'** with jam, jelly, molasses, or honey, fresh tomatoes with sugar, cold cuts of meat, smoked sausage, and, of course, bread. We ate much bread with butter and jam. Another standby for supper was *Kochkäs'*, a homemade cooked cheese, which we ate with buttered bread. Some-times we also had *Handkäs'* ("hand cheese").

A few local German families ate European-style salt herring, but we did not. When I went to school in Mason, I stayed with Mr. and Mrs. Otto Donop, and they sometimes served herring. When we got thirsty from the salty fish, Mr. Donop laughed and said, "Du musst Wasser trinken; der Fisch will schwimmen" ("you have to drink water; the fish wants to swim"). If I hadn't been so young and if beer had not been forbidden among Methodists, he probably would have said, "Du musst Bier trinken."

Fresh fruit was never served with our meals, except tomatoes and occasionally fruit salad. Other fruits like peaches, pears, and plums were usually served cooked, mostly from Kerr, Mason, or Ball

---

* In everyday speech, people in our area all said *Käs'* (pronounced Case) for *Käse* (pronounced Case-uh), both for the simple noun and in compounds like *Schmierkäse* (*Schmierkäs'*), *Kochkäse* (*Kochkäs'*), and *Handkäse* (*Hand-käs'*). I have used the colloquial forms where they seemed appropriate through-out the book.

fruit jars, but sometimes freshly cooked. We also ate home-dried peaches and apricots and store-bought prunes and sliced, dried apples, all well cooked. Sometimes we had desserts, such as cake, cookies, pie, bread pudding, tapioca, and canned or stewed fruit. Ice cream, layer cake, coffee cake, and cookies were served only when visitors came, when we had a *Kaffeeklatsch*, on birthdays, at Christmastime, and at home prayer meetings. Mother always kept a jar of cookies for the kids. We had pies, but no fruit cobblers. I learned to esteem berry cobblers and peach cobblers when I went to East Texas as a schoolteacher. My wife's family and relatives are great cobbler bakers.

We drank mostly plain well water with our meals, but sweet milk for the children and coffee for the adults were seldom missing, especially for breakfast. The milk was often served raw and warm, fresh from the cows. In 1902, when my cousin Jim Stengel was still a small boy, his mother died in Mason from burns received when a coal-oil lamp fell and exploded during a storm, and Jim became a member of our family for a time. Being so accustomed to town ways, he did not like the warm, raw, country milk, so he said, "Ich mag die Milch nicht so roh aus der Kuh" ("I don't like milk so raw from the cow"). We also drank clabber, with sugar added, and plain butter-milk. There was always some homemade sweet wine in the cellar, at least until the Volstead Act prohibiting liquor was passed in 1919, but we drank it only on special occasions, never with meals at the table.

Though Methodist, my father, like most German ethnics, made his own wine by fermenting wild mustang grapes, which grew pro-fusely along the banks of the Willow Creek. One old-timer, A. Weil-bacher, printed a detailed description of the art of wine making. His method is similar to my father's, so I will summarize it in English:

> Crush the ripe grapes by pounding them with a wooden plunger in a tub. Pour the crushed mass into an upright barrel until it is three-fourths full. Now place clean cloth on top and cover the barrel with the lid. A hole must be drilled on one side as close to the bottom as possible and closed with a removable plug. Fermentation will be finished in two to four days. Now tilt the barrel so that the juice will pour into the tub when the plug is removed. Strain out the seeds and hulls and pour the juice

into a forty-four gallon fermentation barrel that is lying horizontally. Pour twenty-two gallons of the new-wine juice into the barrel and add eighty-eight pounds of sugar. To obtain additions for pouring in later, take seventeen to eighteen gallons of water, dissolve one-third or one-half of the eighty-eight pounds of sugar in it, pour this sugar-water into the grape residue left in the first barrel, and stir thoroughly. Repeat fermentation and pouring as above. Then add the rest of the sugar, stir thoroughly, and pour this juice into the barrel, until it is full.

Now the main fermentation will begin, and it will take several weeks. Keep the barrel full to overflowing by adding the remaining juice. Leave the hole open and add juice as long as any waste is expelled. After ten to twelve days, the entry of air should be prevented but the gasses still permitted to escape. Only after the completion of fermentation should the hole be closed. To make possible the escape of the carbon dioxide without the entry of air and vinegar germs, insert a small U-tube and immerse the outside end in water. Around Christmastime, put the wine in another barrel. It will ferment again in spring and turn slightly brown. Then it should be drained off into another barrel or into bottles for storing.

Coffee making was not quite as simple as it is today. During my days we bought roasted Arbuckle coffee beans and ground our own coffee at home in the little coffee grinder on the kitchen wall. We had no percolators or dripolators, so the coffee grains were poured into the water in the coffee pot and boiled, camp-style, for a long time before breakfast, until the liquid was a rich, dark color. It was so black that for dinner and supper Mother just added water to the left-over coffee and the tired grounds. This made a sort of brown-water brew, whose chief virtue was that it didn't keep you awake at night.

In the dining room there was an old-fashioned *Schrank* or "safe." Its top double doors had metal panels, perforated in antique designs. The perforations served both for decoration and ventilation, pointing to the early use of the safe as a pantry or food-storage cabinet. The word *safe* was surely derived from the fact that this cabinet kept the food safe from flies and mice.

The large, cast-iron cookstove or range in the kitchen had its fire box and, to the left, a water heater without plumbing. We had to pour in the water by hand and keep the tank filled. When we wanted to take a bath, we had to dip out the water and pour it into a big washtub or later into the bathtub. Additional water was heated in kettles and pans on top of the stove, where most of our food was cooked. If the fire was not hot enough, we could lift off some of the iron lids and expose the pots and pans directly to the fire below. The baking oven was to the right of the fire box. It served well for baking bread and sweet potatoes, but in summer the whole kitchen became nearly as hot as the stove itself.

In one corner of the kitchen was a large flour box that was opened by raising the large lid. It always held a good supply of flour, some corn meal, and a tin sieve. Flour was bought in fifty-pound cotton sacks, and it was poured, a sack or more at a time, into the flour box, which we called a *Mehlbox.*

Next to the *Mehlbox* was a work table on which great quantities of flour dough were kneaded and shaped into loaves of bread and *Hefekuchen.* The table also served as a general work area, where other foods were prepared and dishes were washed. There was a plain sink with cold running water in the kitchen, but it was used only for washing vegetables and hands, never for dishwashing. The dish-water and table scraps that were not good enough for the dogs were poured into large slop buckets. Also clabber, old milk, or milk from cows that had eaten bitterweed or peppergrass was added and fed to the hogs. One of the regular chores was to carry these heavy buckets of slop to the hog pens and pour the mixture into wooden troughs. This is called "slopping the hogs." Our hogs had an inordinate capacity for slop. I once heard the story about a little pig that could empty a big bucket all alone, and then you could put the whole pig into the empty bucket. I can almost believe that.

Our pepper mill was a square box with a crank on top. We sat down and held it between our knees while we ground the pepper. This was a job for little boys like me. And then there was the old wooden churn with a wooden plunger. Churning, too, was a job delegated to little boys, when there were any. In my days the old plunger had worn such a big hole through the wooden lid that I always got spattered by the cream and buttermilk. My mother made me put an

apron across my lap to catch the spatter. This was something of an
insult to my manly instincts, and it made the task even more dis-
tasteful to me. During the long, long "thump-thump-thump" plunging, I usually peeped in dozens of times to see whether the butter had
finally "made." Usually it hadn't, so the plunging and pounding continued until I was worn out. Later we got a mechanical churn with
gears and a crank. That helped some because I could watch the gears
turn and hear them grind, but it did not speed up the long butter-
making process, which we called *buttern.*

The production and preservation of food was even more difficult
than the cooking and preparation of the meals. The farms and
ranches were self-sustaining for the most part. We bought staple
groceries, such as sugar, flour, salt, pepper, spices, coffee, tea, and
vinegar, in the stores, but we produced most of our food ourselves.
Our vegetable garden and fruit orchard were across the country road
in front of our house, and we grew great quantities and varieties of
vegetables, fruits, and berries.

In the early days my sisters watered the garden from a deep
water hole in the nearby creek. Some dipped water from the pool in
buckets and poured it into a tub across the fence, while others dipped
it from the tub and poured it on the vegetables. After we got a windmill and running water, we could irrigate the garden more easily. In
my teens I became the chief gardener, waterer, rabbit shooter, mole
catcher, and gopher trapper.

My mother and sisters shredded great quantities of cabbage on
a wooden shredder with a double metal blade to make sauerkraut.
They added preservatives like salt and filled large crocks with the
mixture. Then they put lids and rocks on top to press it. They also
made sour pickles and sealed them in jars, and they put gallons of
cucumbers in crocks and preserved them in brine. These were our
Salzgurken ("salt cucumbers"). Sour beets and green beans were
preserved in jars. Also field corn, English peas, and gallons of tomatoes were cooked and preserved in glass jars. We canned chow-chow
and pickled watermelon rinds and green wild grapes used for making
pies. There were long storage shelves in the cool, stone-walled cellar,
where these canned foods, called *Eingemachtes,* were stored. In summer the kitchen resembled a cannery, and the cellar looked like an
army commissary.

We had an opening from the stone cellar stairs to the three-foot space under the floor of the house where we kept Irish potatoes. This was easy work, but storing sweet potatoes, which we called *Patetas* because we had no German word for them, was a man's job. We kept a large box full of dry creek sand in a lean-to built onto the old smokehouse. Each year the sand was dug out, and the sweet potatoes layered in and then covered. The sand kept the potatoes dry and prevented their freezing in winter. Onions were tied up in small bunches and hung by twine in the smokehouse and in the cellar.

We grew our own sweet-potato slips in the garden by burying some potatoes. Then we pulled up the sprouts or slips, and the whole family went to the field and planted them. My father or one of the older boys plowed long rows of potato hills, then one of us chopped holes on top of the hills, and others poured in water by hand and planted the slips. We hauled the water to the field in large barrels on a wagon. Once the slips were established, they grew without watering. When planting Irish or white potatoes, we cut out the eyes or sprouts of the potatoes and planted them in long rows on hills in the garden. At harvesttime, we plowed up the hills and picked the potatoes by hand.

When the tomatoes produced large fall harvests, we picked the last part of the fall crop green, just before the first frost, and carried tubs full into our attic where we spread them on paper to ripen. Thus we often had a supply of fresh tomatoes a month or more after the frost had killed the vines in the garden. Like most German-Texas families, we saved the last English peas, let them get dry, threshed the vines, and put away the dry peas, as we did pinto and butter beans.

In our orchard we had many peach trees, some plum, apricot, pear, and nectarine trees, several thorny date bushes, and a fig tree. There was also a row of blackberries and dewberries. We ate most of our fruit fresh, but we also canned hundreds of quart jars of fruit in sugar syrup. The old adage "We eat what we can, and we can what we can't" certainly applied to us. We also dried some freestone peaches and apricots: we cut them in halves, removed the stones, and placed the halves, inside turned up toward the sun, on a metal roof. When rain threatened, the drying peaches had to be raked off the roof and brought indoors. Some people also dried corn. They cooked the roasting ears, cut off the kernels, and then dried them. In winter this corn was soaked in water, cooked again, and served for dinner.

Pecan trees grew all along the Willow Creek, and the nuts were a good natural food and a valuable cash crop. Sometimes the whole family drove in the wagon to the pecan groves to harvest the pecans. After we cleared the ground under the trees, we spread out wagon sheets, and the men climbed the trees and beat down the nuts. We called this "threshing pecans" in English and *Nüsse dreschen* in German. The nuts that fell on the sheets were easily gathered, but most of them fell in the grass and weeds and had to be picked up by hand. People who gathered pecans, as we did, could easily be identified because everybody got brown fingers and hands. The grown girls did not want to be seen with stained hands, but this did not matter too much because all the Willow Creek girls had brown hands and fingers during October. Actually a girl's stained hands were an unfailing recommendation to any boy looking for a future *Hausfrau*.

We always grew a moderate amount of sorghum cane to make molasses. Uncle August Willmann, who lived three or four miles up the Willow Creek, had a syrup or molasses mill and vat. For a small toll, he helped all the kinfolk and neighbors prepare molasses. We stripped the blades off the cane in the field with homemade wooden machetes, cut the stripped canes with a hand sickle, loaded the cane on the wagon, and hauled it to Uncle August. Father hitched a horse to the molasses mill, and it walked 'round and 'round, while several of us pushed the canes into the metal cylinders. Others carried the buckets of cane juice to the large, flat cooking vat where the juice was boiled. Somebody had to stand by the cooker, stir the juice constantly to keep it from boiling over, and skim it until it became gooey. After carrying off the cane pulp, we poured the finished molasses in large and small cans and took it home.

We also made great quantities of jams and jellies from peaches, plums, apricots, pears, blackberries, wild grapes, tomatoes, wild algerita berries, and watermelons. Watermelon preserves—I don't mean the familiar pickled watermelon rinds—were a Texas-German product, and we called this pulpy jam *Wassermelonenschmier* (literally, "watermelon spread") and smeared it on our bread like *Schmierkäs'*. I have never heard of or seen this product outside of the Texas German Belt. We hauled in wagonloads of watermelons, cut the melons open lengthwise and scraped the meat, seeds, and juice out of the rinds into washtubs. We pressed the juice and pulp through perforated pans placed on top of tall tin containers and poured the pulpy juice into a large copper kettle hung from a pole under a mesquite tree. Then we built a fire under the kettle and let the mass boil all day long, adding juice until early in the afternoon. Scraping the melons and pressing the pulp had to be started early in the morning so that the long boiling process could be finished by evening. So much juice was boiled away that enough natural sugar was concentrated in the jam to preserve it. We put this dark red or brown mass in five- and ten-gallon crocks and ate it by the gallon, three times a day, on bread and butter or with *Schmierkäs'*.

My father kept about a dozen beehives. He set the hives on low tables and benches near a mesquite tree and built a brush arbor over them. When he robbed the bees or captured new swarms, he protected himself with a screen-wire hood, leather gloves, and a thick duck jacket. He made sure that the screen had no holes big enough for bees to crawl through, and he did not fall for the facetious dictum "Rob the bees when they are not at home"; they were always there. He let someone tie cords around the gloves and the sleeves at the wrists to keep out any belligerent bees. We ate some of the honey in the honeycomb, but we squeezed most of it out of the comb and sold the beeswax to the merchants in town.

Milking and feeding the cows, straining and storing the milk, skimming off the cream, churning butter, and curing cheese were such a big enterprise that our ranch operation, from the cowpens to the smokehouse and kitchen, resembled a dairy. Sometimes we milked about twenty cows, not only for our milk, butter, and cheese, but also for the hogs we were fattening. Every morning and night the cows had to be milked. During the day we separated the calves from the cows by putting them in a small pasture while we turned the cows out into a large pasture, and at night we kept the cows and calves in separate pens. At milking time we let in only a few cows at a time, one for each milker. The calves "primed" the cows, and after the cows had "let down" their milk, we tied the calves until we had gotten our share of milk. We always left enough for the calves. Here is a little ditty that we recited sometimes while we milked:

Strip, strap, stroll;
Ist der Eimer bald voll?

(Strip, strop, strull;
Will the bucket soon be full?)

These lines appear in Grimm's fairy tale "Des Schneiders Däumer-ling Wanderschaft" ("Thumbling's Travels"), from which we memo-rized it in school.

Sometimes a cow kicked the bucket—I mean it literally, kicked the bucket—or trampled the milk pail all out of shape. Those were trying times, and many a mild and meek German Methodist lost his temper, at least temporarily, and began speaking in strange tongues while he picked up the bent bucket and kicked the cow "tit for tat," "a tooth for a tooth," and "an eye for an eye." We should have known that range cows are only half-domesticated and not at all civilized. Much later we got a few docile Jersey milch cows, and they set a good example for the white-faced and brindle range cows. This cow-kicking topic brings to mind the story about the pious Quaker who, when the cow kicked him, said, "I cannot curse thee or beat thee, but I can sell thee to a Baptist, and he will eat thee."

There was a long shelf built against the rail fence, and we placed an array of milk pails and buckets on the high shelf until the milking was finished. In the early days, when my parents had a house-ful of daughters, the girls were all milkmaids, and they kept their fingernails cut short. The range cows would certainly have taken ex-ception to long, sharp nails.

After the milking, we took the big buckets of milk to the milk chest in the smokehouse. This chest was an open case with three or four shelves. On top was a water trough, and cotton curtains hung down from it on all sides. These were kept moist by the water seep-ing through the cloth. This was our homemade refrigeration. The milk did not get cold, but the evaporation of the water kept it cool enough to let the cream rise and cause the rest of the milk to change to clabber (*dicke Milch*: "thick milk") without getting too sour.

We skimmed off the cream and churned it into butter, then took some of the clabber, poured it into a cheesecloth bag, and hung it out to let the whey drain into a slop bucket. The chinaberry tree from which the bag of clabber hung was our "cheese tree." When enough liquid had drained, we took down the bag, poured the fresh, home-made cottage cheese into a bowl, and stirred in salt and some sour cream. This was our *Schmierkäs'*. We always put a spoonful of jam, preserves, jelly, honey, or molasses on the cheese and ate it with or without butter and bread. We ate *Schmierkäs'* and honey so much that we could claim we lived in the land of milk and honey.

All the families of the German ethnic group in the Hill Country of Texas and, no doubt, elsewhere also made *Kochkäse* ("cooked cheese"). It is really quite easy to make. Take some cottage cheese or curd, press it several days until it gets fairly dry, crumble it, add salt, pepper, and caraway seed, place it in thin layers on large plat-ters or cake pans, and let it ripen. It produces a potent odor, but as a harbinger of the *Kochkäs'*, this smell is not too bad. After the cheese has ripened enough, it is boiled a short while over a moderately hot stove, and there is your *Kochkäse*. It can be eaten hot, in melted state, or it can be poured into a bowl, let cool and congeal, to be sliced and eaten with fresh homemade bread and butter.

Another kind of cheese is called *Handkäse*, literally, "hand cheese," but better known in English as ball cheese. It too is made from pressed and dried cottage cheese or curd. Salt, pepper, and caraway seed are added. Then the cheese is shaped by hand into balls about the size of baseballs, and set on boards to cure in the shape of mountain peaks. When a soft, golden rind is formed, the cheese is ready for eating. Too much ripening and too thick a yellow rind may make the cheese a bit strong for refined and delicate tastes.

Providing meat in summer was a difficult matter because we had no adequate refrigeration. Even so, there were several choices. The simplest was, of course, to fry a chicken or two. To have nice, clean chickens to eat we kept several in a coop, a sort of death row, and fattened them. At the proper time my mother or one of my older sisters pulled out a couple of chickens and unceremoniously chopped off their heads. The place of execution was the old woodpile, where there were plenty of chopping blocks and the ground was covered with tree bark and wood chips. This kept the beheaded chickens from wallowing in the sand and getting their bare necks gritty.

When I was big enough to perform the dreaded decapitation, I inherited this job from my sisters. It was always an unpleasant act, and I tried to make it as efficient as possible. I selected a large log and made a wire hook for the chicken's head. Then I held the chicken by its legs and wings, slipped the head into the noose-like wire hook, stretched the neck across the execution block by pulling on the chicken with one hand, and chopped off the head with a hatchet. Before the installation of the hook, I had missed too often because the chickens saw the hatchet come down and jerked their heads away just in time. I always wanted to shoot the chickens with my twenty-two rifle, but everybody objected. So the execution by hatchet continued.

The second choice for summer meat was a small quadruped like a sheep or mutton. Killing a sheep was much worse than beheading a chicken, and I will spare you the details. Of course, being cattle raisers and ranch people, we wanted beef in summer. The problem was that no single family, no matter how large (we were an even dozen for several years, plus one or two farmhands, can eat a whole beef in summer. For that reason, my family entered into a four-way agreement with the families of my uncles Ernst Jordan, Heinrich Jordan, and August Willmann. By this agreement the families took turns slaughtering a beef, and each family received one quarter. Inasmuch as the families were large, a quarter of beef could be handled, but even so it took some planning. My mother knew how to roast all the fresh meat and store the surplus in a crock in a mass of grease. This roasted beef in congealed lard kept quite well in our cool cellar.

We ate no fresh pork in summer, but when the weather became cooler in autumn, we sometimes killed a shoat and baked the hams and shoulders. This was done before the big hog-killing time in winter. When the cold winter weather came, we butchered once or twice during December, January, or February. This meant slaughtering four or five fat hogs and a head of beef or two. It was unpleasant work, and I would never have used the phrase "a hog-killing *good* time." After the hog was shot and bled, it was dragged on a wooden, horse-drawn sled to the old mesquite tree behind the house, where water was boiling in the big copper kettle. The hog was scalded and the bristles scraped off. Then a singletree was hooked on the hind legs, and the hog was pulled up by means of a rope pulley and dissected. We kept the heart, liver, and tongue to be cooked for the

Leberwurst ("liver sausage"). The hams and shoulders were cut for making cured and smoked ham, and the side meat was cut from the ribs and made into bacon.

We had a table in the stone smokehouse where we peppered and salted down the hams and sides of hog and let the meat cool and the seasoning soak in well. Then we suspended the ham and bacon from the rafters by means of grass twine and smoked and dried the meat thoroughly, along with the sausage. We used oak chips and bark to produce the smoke.

While the hams and sides of bacon started curing in salt and pepper, we processed the rest of the meat. Some bone meat was cut up to be eaten as pot roast. The fatty parts of the pork together with the livers, hearts, tongues, jowls, legs, and pig knuckles were put in the big copper kettle and boiled along with some beef liver, heart, and tongue. The less fatty pork was mixed with beef for cured or hard sausage.

A grass-fattened beef was usually slaughtered at the same time, and all hands had to be on deck or, better said, in the yard and under the trees. We cut or sawed the beef into quarters and let it cool. The best cuts were used for steaks and roasts, and the poorer grades were cut from the bones and put into the sausage along with similar cuts of pork. The cowhide was salted and rolled into a ball to be sold in town.

We always made two kinds of sausage (*Wurst*): cooked sausage and cured sausage. Although we did not claim that "our Wurst is the best," as the people of New Braunfels and Castroville do now, we certainly knew that our sausage was excellent and tasty. All the meat intended for cooked sausage was boiled in the copper pot. Then the bones were removed, and the mixed pork and beef were ground up in a sausage grinder, seasoned, and stuffed into sausage casings or jackets. We tied one end of the casings and stuffed them with cooked sausage meat. One of us turned the crank geared to the stuffer, while another held the casings on the snout and punctured the emerging sausage with a fork to avoid air bubbles. A third person tied the ends to make sausage loops or rings. With all these sausage loops around us, nobody would have thought of the answer to "The Old Farmer's Riddle," which reads, "Everything has an end, but what has two?"

The answer to the riddle is "a sausage," but this was not our kind of sausage.

Sometimes a casing burst, and the filling squirted out on the table. The temptation was great to make the sausage meat squirt out a yard or two on the table after the casing burst. This always produced laughter by the kids and a reprimand by our elders. All the while, other members of the family were cutting meat, mixing, seasoning, and grinding it, and carrying sausage to the big kettle to be boiled again.

After the finished sausage was boiled in the same water in which the meat had been boiled, there remained a rich, soupy liquid. Into this sausage juice we poured some leftover sausage meat, some cornmeal, flour, and seasoning and boiled it until the mass thickened. This preparation was then poured into rectangular pans and left to congeal in the shape of loaves of bread. This was our *Pannas*. After the mass set, we cut off slices and fried them with cooked sausage. The sausage and *Pannas* were on the greasy side, but we liked them. *Pannas* is very similar to Philadelphia scrapple, and the word is related to Pennsylvania-Dutch *Ponhaws*, the anglicized form of the word derived from the Low German *Pannhas*. This is *Pfannhase* in standard High German, and it means "pan rabbit," indicating that originally, hundreds of years ago, rabbit was used instead of pork. We also rendered large quantities of lard. The fatty trimmings of pork were cut into small pieces and boiled in the large kettle. The leftover pieces became crisp like bacon and were called cracklings. The melted lard was poured into large buckets and crocks and saved for later use.

Making cured sausage was a process similar to the preparation of cooked sausage, but the meat was raw. It was ground, mixed, seasoned, and stuffed into casings. The proportion of beef, approximately two-thirds, was much higher than in the cooked liverwurst. The seasoning was primarily salt, black pepper, either ground or in whole peppercorns, and saltpeter. The sausage loops were hung on poles or old broom handles, laid across the tie beams beneath the rafters of the smokehouse, and then thoroughly smoked and dried, along with the ham, bacon, and peppered beef.

The Texas-German smoked sausage we made was similar to the

sausage that is still prepared in the German settlements of the Hill Country. It can be bought in many towns like New Braunfels, Fredericksburg, and Mason. Some of it is marketed extensively, for example the well-known Opa's Country Style Smoked Sausage, made in Fredericksburg. I am tempted to call this Hill Country product "Ger.-Mex.-Tex. sausage" because there is an influence of Texas-Mexican seasoning. Certainly the Texas-German *Wurst* is seasoned more highly than similar sausage made in Germany. If it is to be eaten relatively fresh, it should be pan broiled or oven baked. This brings out the most delicious flavor. Later, when it has been smoked and dried more thoroughly, it can be eaten without cooking, like commercial summer sausage, especially when it is all-beef.

To make peppered beef, we dipped strips of the meat into boiling water for a few minutes, put salt and black pepper on it, and smoked it a long time. We rescued it before it got as hard and dry as Mexican jerky, but it became dry enough to carry it in our saddlebags.

After the ham, bacon, sausage, and peppered beef were sufficiently smoked and cured, we carried them on the poles to the cellar and hung them on the joists overhead. When summertime approached, my mother and the girls put all the remaining sausage and cured meat away in crocks and poured melted lard over the meat, so that it would keep all summer. As we needed sausage, bacon, or ham in the hot season, they dug it out of the lard mixture, and we ate the sausage in the dried and cured state, just as summer sausage is eaten. The lard mixture added flavor and juiciness to the meat.

Before the time of modern transportation, the choice and production of food was determined largely by environment and only slightly by the taste of the people who produced it. However, the preservation and preparation of food usually reflected more strongly the background of various ethnic groups. In our case there was still a distinct German influence, but at the same time we also adopted many Anglo-Texan foods, as we have seen above.

4

Father Was a Ranchman

My father had a diversified farm operation, but he was primarily a ranchman. By the time he entered the livestock industry in the 1880's, most ranches were enclosed by barbwire fences, so he could begin selective breeding. He improved his original mixed-Longhorn livestock by crossbreeding with Durham (Shorthorn) bulls and later with Herefords. The crossbred Durham cows gave more milk and raised bigger calves than any others, and the Herefords were the best range cattle of the time.

Once the white-faced Herefords took hold on the ranches, most ranchmen began to raise this breed, and it became almost a patriotic duty to do so. My father never raised purebred cattle of any kind, but Brother Frank was so carried away by his interest in registered livestock that he developed a deep but unfulfilled desire to travel to England to see Hereford, the native shire of the ancestors of his purebred herds, and he became deeply involved with the Texas Hereford Association.

Good cattle raisers know their herds well, even the individual cows. To me all cows looked alike, just as the thousands of people at a football game look alike to me, but my father and my brothers had their cows catalogued in their minds. "That calf with the red spots around its eyes is out of that old red cow," my father might say, for example.

"Yes, that's right, she always drops calves like that," added Brother Dan. "She has a lot of Durham in her. I bet she'll raise another fat calf."

Brother Frank spied another calf and said: "That little calf over there is out of the old, line-back cow. She always drops calves with too much white. We need a better Hereford bull to get rid of those white skunk stripes."

I put in my two-bits worth by grunting "huh, huh," and Brother Milton added: "Yeah, I'd rather have a red-neck cow than one of those skunk backs. That white-booted bull has sired too many leggy calves with white backs and tails. Let's send him to Fort Worth."

Range cattle had to be checked frequently to see that all were there and well. When a sick animal or one with screwworms was found, it was driven to the pens for doctoring. To check our cattle we rode for long hours all over the pastures, counted the animals, and looked carefully at each head of the herd. Things have become much simpler now. Modern pickup-truck cattle raisers have trained their herds to come running for inspection when they hear the car horn. The trick is, of course, to have some feed ready to reward the co-operating cows. In years past, car drivers honked their horns at cattle in the road to make them get out of the way. Now they don't dare honk. If they do, the whole herd will come running, block the road, and moo for a handout. My father used his own technique when he put out salt and called his herd with a loud "Sook! Sook! Sook!"

Rounding up a big herd of cattle was always an exciting experience. After several small herds were driven together, say at a watering place, the whole herd was moved toward the pens. Letting out a crescendo of moos, the herd was urged along by our yelling and cracking of bull whips. One man rode on each side, and one or two at the back. Occasionally a rebellious calf or yearling broke away, and a wild race started. Usually the horse and rider could outrun the unwilling yearling, but in thick brush or timber many a steer escaped. As we approached the home pens, the smarter beasts became suspicious and made further wild dashes for freedom. By this time, however, there was little chance of a successful stampede because we had "out-foxed" or "out-cowed" the animals by building our fences in a funnel-shaped approach to the cowpens.

These cattle roundups faintly resembled the old open-range cow hunts my father used to tell us about, but they were shorter and required no chuck wagon and supplies. Some good cow ponies, saddles, and experienced riders were the main things needed, and it was relatively easy to find and round up the herds on thousand-acre ranches.

Because ranching in Texas was primarily Anglo and Hispanic-Mexican and originally foreign to all German settlers, much of the ranch vocabulary was new. There were no German words for *ranch,* and *roundup*. As a result, hundreds of English words were taken over into the settlers' German with some germanizing. This resulted in nouns like *die Ränsch* ("ranch"), *der Päster* ("pasture"), *die Fens* ("fence"), *die Stacheldrahtfens* ("barbwire fence"), *die Geht* ("gate"), *das Rop* ("rope"), *die Penne* ("pen"), and *die Kuhpenne* ("cowpen"). Verbs too were borrowed, for example, *ropen* ("to rope"), *aufrounden* ("to round up"), *Vieh dippen* ("to dip cattle"), and *dehornen* ("to dehorn").* Incidentally, it is interesting that, although the German settlers had no background of open-range, large-scale ranching in Europe, some of them like the Klebergs, Schreiners, and Scharbauers became great cattle barons of Texas.

Roping cattle out in the open pastures is inadvisable, and all smart ranchmen quit this practice long ago. Most roping is a sport now, mainly at rodeos and roping contests. During my ranch days there was, however, still much roping going on, especially in the cow lots. Some men and boys developed great roping skills, and others mixed in a little gratuitous showmanship. The flamboyant ones went through some fancy swinging of their lassos around their heads before they finally threw their ropes. My brothers Dan and Frank developed a quick throw, and this usually caught their victims unaware and brought them down while the show boys were still fanning the air with their lariats. I always admired those quick throws, just as I enjoy the quick delivery of a modern baseball pitcher rather than one of those old-time windmill windups. As for me, I managed to develop the windup, but I never learned accurate delivery, and that goes for baseball as well as roping.

Brother Frank once had a painful accident while roping a big yearling with a Manila hemp lasso. These ropes were very strong, but they were also dangerous to human hands. When Frank roped his yearling, he was wearing leather gloves to keep the rope from burning his hands while it was sliding through. He managed to throw a successful lasso around the animal's neck, but the rope got tangled around two of his right-hand fingers. The yearling jerked him down

---

* I have germanized the spelling of these words; elsewhere I give their English forms to aid readers' recognition of them. The final *e* in the anglicized form was not pronounced and so does not appear on the German form, where a final *e* would always be pronounced. Actually, there is no standard spelling for these germanized English words.

and dragged him until the two fingers came off with the glove. After a long, painful wait, the doctor finally came from town, and with a hacksaw he cut off the protruding bone of one finger from which the flesh had been stripped away. Then he sewed up the stubs of the two fingers, and Frank had to go though life and World War I with only three fingers on his right hand. Fortunately, these were his thumb and his writing and trigger fingers. Frank was the most accident-prone of us all. Once he and Dan were running their horses across a mesquite flat when Frank's horse, good old Kate, stepped in a gopher hole and turned a somersault. Frank landed safely, but Kate fell with her head turned under her shoulder and broke her neck. So Frank and Dan walked home, leading one horse with two saddles on it.

My brother-in-law Edwin Donop also had a bad accident, in which he lost one eye. A cow had such big teats that her calf could not suckle. Edwin roped the cow in the pasture, wound the rope around a tree, and milked her, while Frank held the rope. When Edwin tried to remove the loop of the rope from the cow's head, she hit him in the face with one of her horns, and he lost an eye.

I, too, had my little brush with danger, when I was thirteen years old. I went to the pasture with an ear of corn and a rope to catch one of the horses. Most of them were too sly to cooperate, but I could usually catch old Blue or Dolly. This time Dolly came up to eat the corn, while I tied a rope around her neck and looped it around her nose to form a halter, as I had always done. Then I jumped on and rode bareback while I drove the other horses home. Suddenly they began to run like wild mustangs, and I could not hold Dolly back. The chase went faster and faster until I fell off. I was knocked out completely but fortunately not seriously hurt.

Talking about ranch accidents reminds me of a little German ditty that my sister-in-law Dina Treibs Jordan relayed to me. I think she got it from Joe Molberg of Fredericksburg. It sounds like a humorous mock epitaph, but I never saw it on a gravestone:

> Durch einen Ochsenstoss
> Flog ich in Abrahams Schoss;
> Ich ging zur ewig'n Ruh
> Durch dich, du Rindvieh du.
>
> (By a wild ox I was gored,
> So to Abraham's bosom I soared;

To eternal rest I flew
Through you, dumb ox, through you.)

When Texas cattlemen got all fired up about tick fever, we built a dipping vat with pens and chutes and dipped our cattle to kill the ticks. We drove the cattle into a big pen and from there into a small pen with a chute that led to the concrete vat with the dip mixture. Most cows were unwilling to take the plunge into the vat and its awful stench. As soon as we got them trapped in the chute, we rammed poles through the chute behind them. At this stage, most cows saw that they had no choice and plunged into the vat in desperation. Then they swam the length of the big tub and climbed out on the steps at the other end. There was a small dripping pen there with a concrete floor. The cows stood there and snorted until the dip mixture had drained back into the vat.

Occasionally a few suspicious cows refused to take the big leap. For them we had a little "persuader," an electric prodding rod that administered a mild but sudden shock when we pushed the button and touched the cattle on their hindquarters with the rod. This was not as bad as beating on the poor animals or twisting their tails. One thing is sure, every cow that got the shock treatment took off like lightning and hit the dip mixture so hard that much of it splashed out.

Sometimes a calf got turned around in the chute or in the vat. For this emergency we had a pole with a hook on one end. We caught the calf by his neck with the hook, turned him around, and helped him along toward the exit. After the dipping we released the cattle, and the whole herd took off like African wildebeests. In a few days the ticks dropped off, man and beast were relieved, and Mr. Capps, the tick inspector, was satisfied.

In addition to tick infestation, there was the constant problem with screwworms. When we found infested animals, we drove them home to the pens and poured screwworm killer into the stinking wounds. Soon the larvae died and dropped off, but continued treatment was required to prevent reinfestation.

Some cattle doctoring was strictly quackery, but most of the animals survived in spite of it. One bit of well-intentioned nonsense was the old effort to prevent blackleg by cutting slits in the hides of the animals and inserting chunks of asafetida. Other so-called remedies were to bleed the sick animals by cutting gashes in the roofs of their mouths so they would swallow their own blood or to drill holes in their horns or dehorn them when they had "hollow horn." These spurious remedies were not only cruel, but useless at best and in some cases harmful or fatal.

Horse doctoring was just about as quackish as cattle doctoring. If a horse had swinney (German *Schwinne*), you could cut a slit in the horsehide on the shoulder and insert a two-bit coin, or a dime if you were stingy. This was supposed to cure the atrophy of the shoulder muscles. One treatment for distemper was to drive the horses into the chute and hold buckets of a smoldering preparation under their noses and make them breathe the vile vapor.

The thing I disliked most about ranch life, and something I could never do, was the pocket-knife surgery: castrating little lambs, calves, and pigs, marking animals by clipping out bits of their ears, and cutting off the lambs' tails. Branding cattle with hot irons was another disagreeable task. We drove the animals into a chute and heated the branding irons in the coals of a wood fire. Then we pressed the hot irons firmly on the live cowhide. In my imagination I can still smell the burned hair and hide and hear the poor animals bawl in pain.

My father's brand was a plain J with a bar underneath, applied on the left hip—a small, simple brand, less cruel than some of the large, pretentious ones. We smeared axle grease on the fresh brand to ease the pain and help heal the hide. Weeks later the branded area peeled off and left permanent scars.

When it was time to sell or market—I almost said "harvest"— cattle, we rounded up our herds and sold some of the animals to cattle buyers, just as the early cattlemen had sold their longhorns to the trail drivers. During my days on the ranch we sold two-year-old steers to buyers like Henry Hoerster, John Hasse, and Daniel Bickenbach. Mason County never had a railroad, so these buyers drove their herds to Brady and shipped them by rail to the Fort Worth market for slaughtering in the Swift and Armour packinghouses. Sometimes we shipped our own cattle and sold them through the cattle commission companies.

I remember in the late teens my uncle Ernst Jordan and I accompanied a shipment of cattle to Fort Worth. We drove our combined herds along the main road to Mason, then through the town, and farther on to Brady. This was a two-day cattle drive, and several of my brothers and cousins helped. The highway right-of-way was fenced, and driving the cattle was relatively simple. We guided them along one of the side fences and kept them off the roadway, just in case a car might come along. We had several watering places along the way, and we rented a roadside pasture for the night, where our cattle had good grazing and water. This was at about the halfway point to Brady.

We brought along a chuck wagon with food, water, bedding, and feed for the horses. Our camping place was near the rented pasture, and we pitched camp on a rocky knoll by the road. There we slept under the stars by our wagon and our saddles. The second day, having risen early, we managed to arrive at the Brady loading pens. After we watched the livestock being put into the railroad cattle cars, everybody except Uncle Ernst and me started back for Mason County. A free ride in the caboose was provided for us cattle shippers, and Uncle Ernst and I crawled in and took a long, uncomfortable ride to the city. I can still hear the all-night, "clickety-clack" sound of the wheels on the iron rails.

At Fort Worth we saw our cattle in the livestock pens, took a tour of the Armour and Company slaughter house, and made a short visit to the zoo and Forest Park, while the commission company sold our cattle. Then we picked up our checks and started back home. This time we got to ride in a regular train coach.

In good or normal years our cattle lived off the land. The grass in Mason County is very nourishing, even when it is dormant in winter. Only in the drought years did we have to feed our livestock. We raised our own sorghum-cane hay and corn-top fodder and stored them in haylofts and haystacks. We also fed some cottonseed and grain, and in the severe 1917–1918 drought we bought cake and other commercially prepared feeds that were shipped in.

There was an abundant growth of pear cactus on our land, and we used it for cow feed in dry years. The thorns and spines had to be burned off before cactus could be fed to the cows. In the early days we built large bonfires in the pasture and held the cactus plants over the flames with pitchforks until the thorns were burned off. The cows stood around and mooed for the broiled cactus, while the pitchfork men stood half-roasted in front and cold in back. Later, coal-oil-fueled pear burners came into use, and they lightened the work considerably. Some of our cattle developed the cactus habit to such a degree that they ate raw cactus, thorns and all. Eating thorns made their mouths so sore they could not eat normally, and they half starved to death if we did not take them away from the cactus.

My father gave each of his children a heifer when we were in our early teens. He let us select our own animals and start our own herds. Mine was a pretty, dark-red heifer with a fair face. As the years went by, my heifer multiplied, and I recorded my own brand, J4, so designated because I was the fourth son.

In contrast to cattle breeding, sheep raising and hog ranching were relatively small operations. The practice of combining sheep raising with cattle ranching was introduced into the Hill Country by German settlers, and sheep raising was started locally by Ottmar von Behr of Sisterdale, Kendall County. My father's interest in sheep went back to his childhood, when he had herded his father's flock. He believed a small flock of sheep should be run on the range along with cattle. He said that sheep eat weeds, while cattle prefer grass. In this way the sheep purify the grass and complement the cattle. It is what we might now call symbiosis, a mutually beneficial living together.

Sheepherding was no longer necessary on our fenced-in ranch in the twentieth century, so we turned our flock out in the pasture, but we put them in a pen every night because of marauding wolves, coyotes, wildcats, and dogs. Even so, there were some daytime losses. The sheep were trained to come home in the late afternoon. Sometimes we had to hunt a few stragglers and we could easily find them by the sound of their bells.

Sheep usually stay in flocks or groups, and they follow their leader blindly. Thus it was easy to count the sheep every evening. We let one or two leaders run through a gate and then held the gate open only slightly, so that the sheep ran through in single file while one of us counted them. Most of the sheep took a victorious leap after they squeezed through the narrow opening. If any were missing, we went out in search immediately.

I remember one exciting rescue. Our sheep had to cross the Willow Creek on their way to and from the pasture. Normally the creek had a dry bed or flowed only a small stream. However, when heavy rains fell, the creek filled with water and sometimes went on a rampage. On this occasion the creek took a rise during the day, but we could still ride through on horseback. The sheep, however, wouldn't cross the stream. Sheep can swim, but they will not venture into deep water on their own. We tried to drive them into the water, but they would not go. Then we caught a few of them and pushed them into the water, but they came right back. Finally we roped the big old bellwether and pulled him by horse into the rushing stream, and the rest of them, in true sheep fashion, followed. The sheep were carried downstream a hundred yards or more, but all landed safely, shook their fleecy pelts, and let us drive them home.

During lambing time we put the ewes in a small pasture where we could keep an eye on them. When a ewe gave birth to a lamb or two and accidentally got separated from her young, she would not accept her own offspring. A cow will always accept her calf or even take on an extra calf, but ewes are disconcertingly obstinate about this. I remember that several times, when a lamb died, we tried to get its mother ewe to accept an orphan lamb, only to be met by stubborn resistance. Even after we hung the skinned fleece of her dead lamb over the orphan to be adopted, the ewe would still refuse. As a result we usually fed several rejected lambs from bottles. Once I had twin lambs that I raised on bottles, and, in spite of the fact that I really hated sheep because of their stupidity, their snotty noses, and their offensive odor, the twin lambs became my pets. I still have a picture of myself as an eleven-year-old boy holding my arms around the necks of my favorite lambs.

We raised sheep primarily for their wool. In late spring we drove the flock into a pen, caught the sheep one by one, and sheared them with hand shears. Then we rolled up the wool, tied it into individual fleeces, stuffed them into large, suspended wool sacks, and sewed the sacks up at the top. Then we hauled the wool to town, where we sold it to the country-produce firms, which were subsidiaries of dry-goods and grocery stores.

Hog ranching is mostly a thing of the past. Now little pigs are usually raised in pens and then transferred to "hog parlors," where they grow up in hygienic luxury and are fattened by automatic feeding. In the early days the German settlers in the Hill Country raised swine in large numbers on the ranches, and the hogs lived on roots, acorns, and pecans. Grandfather Jordan had large droves of hogs on his ranchland in the 1880's, and he and his family slaughtered hogs by the hundreds and sold the ham, bacon, sausage, and lard. Until about 1916 or 1917 my father, too, raised from fifty to one hundred hogs in his pastures. In good years the range hogs fattened on mast and pecans. If they were penned occasionally, they remained tame, but if they were left to fend for themselves, they became wild and sometimes vicious.

We usually kept at least one good hog dog to help us round up these semiwild animals. The best one we ever had was old Bob, or Leo as we called him sometimes. He was brave and aggressive like a lion and helped in rousting the hogs out of the underbrush. He knew how to nip the hogs on their hams and chase them out into the open where we could handle them on horseback. Sometimes he was carried away by his enthusiasm and his desire to please his master.

On one occasion he encountered a big boar that had long, sharp tusks. When the hogs did not respond to his barking and nipping on their hams, Bob tried to clamp his teeth on the boar's ear and hold him. This sort of attack usually persuaded the meanest hogs to co-operate, provided the dog was agile enough to keep from being slashed. After all, hogs' ears grow dangerously close to their tusks. Bob knew this as well as any hog dog, but in his zeal he must have made a false move, and the boar ripped open his belly. This was a near-fatal injury, but we took him home and sewed him up. He got well but went through the rest of his life with a long abdominal scar and a terrible temper and disposition. After the accident, Bob was even better with hogs than before because he tempered his bravery with caution and cunning. Speaking of hog dogs prompts me to add that *hog dog* literally would be *Schweinehund* in German, but we never called Bob a *Schweinehund* because in German that is a curse word, about as bad as calling somebody "a dirty dog," "a yellow cur," or "an S.O.B."

My father tried to keep his range hogs tame and manageable. He fed the brood sows and their pigs until the shoats weighed about thirty pounds and then turned them out to pasture. Later he often carried ears of corn in a tow sack tied to his saddle and rode out to check the hogs, calling loudly "Wootchie, wootchie, wootchie" until they came out of the timber. Then he fed them corn while he inspected them. In bad years the hogs had to be rounded up and fed at home. Even before 1920 swine ranching had declined so much that we turned more and more to pen feeding and domesticating the hogs. We upgraded our herd by introducing Poland-China, Duroc-Jersey, and Berkshire breeds, but my father did not like Berkshire hogs because their snouts are turned up so much they cannot root very well.

I remember one episode from the days of the wild range hogs. With old Bob's aid, we had rounded up a drove of vicious swine. After we penned them, a hog buyer from town came to buy and haul them off. As he started to walk into the pen, my father warned him that these were wild range hogs, but he replied, "I ain't scared o' no darn hogs I ever seen," and walked right into the pen. The hogs immediately raised their bristles, roared in throaty, gargled growls, and took out like wild javelinas after the city guy. One big boar with long, sharp tusks led the attack, followed by the whole herd of bellowing hogs. The evil spirits that entered the swine in the Bible story must have possessed these beasts. Our hog buyer turned on his heels and headed for the fence. When he saw that this was a high, stone fence, he turned sharply to the right. This slowed down the hogs, and he was able to reach the slat gate and climb it just as the big boar crashed into the gate about six inches below him. Later we managed to drive the hogs into the chute and load them, and the buyer left with a healthy respect for wild boars.

Horses were an absolute necessity on the ranch and farm. We had some multipurpose animals, but others were specialists: cow ponies, buggy and surrey horses, and draft animals for wagons and plows. My father raised a few for our own use, but he did not consider this a profitable enterprise because horses have an insatiable urge to paw at fences. Sometimes one of them almost cut off a foot when caught in a barbwire fence, and such cuts healed slowly and often left a horse permanently lame.

All the horses had their own names and personalities. There were old Blue, the would-be racehorse and balker; Schimmel, whose name meant Gray; Koli, the black kicker; Jerry, the big wagon and plow horse, who could also pull our heavy, two-span buggy alone; Maude, the water guzzler, who put her whole mouth up to her nostrils into the water while she half emptied the wooden trough; Dolly, the quick and jolly saddle horse; Nellie, the agile pacer; Wilson, our staid and dignified trotter; and Bryan, the inveterate show off. We also had one donkey for several years, but he was as stubborn as the soil, as unpredictable as any politician, and about as useful on the ranch as a bicycle.

Chicken raising was small-fry business, and my mother raised them mostly for our home meat supply and for eggs as well as for the little "chicken change" she got from sales of fryers and eggs. We raised mostly Plymouth Rocks and Rhode Island Reds. They were not the best egg layers, but they were big and meaty. My father had a cattleman's grudge against them, partly because he did not like fried chicken. Then, too, he had several unpleasant encounters in the barnyard. The chickens were always underfoot, and sometimes he would trip over a hen. They were into everything and ate his livestock feed. If he and Mother ever had a serious argument, it was over chickens.

We also raised a few turkeys and ducks, but no geese, no pigeons, no guineas, and no peafowls. Our neighbors, the Standkes, had enough peacocks for the whole neighborhood, and we could hear their cries at a distance of one-half mile or more. Turkeys were less objectionable. Of course, they made enough "gobble-gobble" and "put-put-put" noise, but they strayed off into the pasture and were not always under foot. One side benefit of raising turkeys was their snake warning. Whenever there was a lot of turkey "put-put-put" calling, it was advisable to look for a rattlesnake nearby. Baby turkeys, though, are curious and dumb about snakes. They go "put, put, put" and walk right up to a rattler. While they turn their heads from one side to another, the snake has a good chance to strike and swallow them.

Most farms and ranches have many cats, ostensibly to catch rats and mice but also to be pets for the girls. Some of our cats were good mousers, but others were so well fed that they turned up their noses at rats and mice. Dogs were more to my liking, and we always kept several watch dogs, cow dogs, hog dogs, and hunting dogs. In addition to old Bob, the hog dog, there were Teddy and Russell. I think Teddy was a half-breed Border collie, and he and his partners were good cow dogs as well as pets for us boys.

In the first quarter of the twentieth century nobody ever thought of brush clearing and grass planting, but we did try to control the cockleburs. The Willow Creek would have been badly infested with these plants if we had not pulled them up or cut them down each year. It was impractical to raise sheep in a pasture with cockleburs because it is all but impossible to remove the burs from the wool. Also horses would get cockleburs in their tails and manes, and the burs could not be removed without clipping the manes and thinning out the tails. For cattle, too, cockleburs in tails and long hair were troublesome. So there was nothing else to do but pull up the cockle-bur plants before the burs developed. We had to do this every year because some ranchmen upstream did not control burs on their property, and the seeds washed down to us. Pulling up cockleburs was a hot, mean job. It was one of the things that caused me not to want to be a ranchman on the Willow Creek.

Providing water for the animals was not easy. In addition to the two or three wells by the house, we had a number of surface-water tanks, but during severe droughts they dried up. A more reliable source of ranch water was the Willow Creek. It flowed a little stream in the cooler seasons of the year, but it was dry most of the summer. So we dug in the sand of the creek bed down to the water level with hand-operated, horse-drawn scrapers. Then we set wooden boxes without bottoms into the water and poured sand against the outside. When the water level went down later, we scraped deeper and reset the boxes.

Barbwire fences were easier to build than rock fences and much better than the early zigzag or snake-rail fences, but they too had to be rebuilt constantly, not only to repair the ravages of time and age but also to reconstruct the damage done by floods and fighting bulls.

Two of our ranches lay astride the Willow Creek, and a third one spread across a tributary, the Little Willow. This meant we had seven or eight creek fences that washed away in floods. When the whole fence was washed away, we set up the posts again, stretched the wire with a block and tackle, and stapled the wire on firmly. To avoid frequent fence repairs in the creek, we also had a few water gaps. These were made of wood slats with gaps between the boards. They were suspended from heavy wire cables overhead. In high water they floated without breaking, and they could easily be put back in place after the flood. Fence posts were cut by ax, mostly from mesquite trees. The heavier ones furnished the corner posts, and the tall ones were used for gateposts.

Gates were installed in the fences at every road intersection. Slat gates that were hung by metal hinges and fastened by chains or wire loops on top could be opened easily. If the chain or wire fasteners were properly installed, you could easily open and close the gates without dismounting. Most horses were trained to stand parallel to the gate, but if you had to lean over too much, the horse might jump, and you would hit the ground, head first. One of the unwritten laws of ranching is that you must always close all gates carefully.

Farming was primarily a sideline to our ranching enterprise. To be sure, we did sometimes raise small quantities of cash crops, such as cotton, but our main purpose was to raise feed for our livestock. We cultivated four small fields, the largest one no more than twenty acres. The chief grain crops were corn, wheat, oats, rye, and milo maize. We also raised some speckled cowpeas, peanuts, sorghum cane, and Sudan grass.

By the 1900's we had a good supply of horse-drawn farm implements: turning plows, riding cultivators, sweeps, single and double harrows, riding planters, mowers, rakes, and corn-stalk cutters. In spite of good horsepower, the operation of these implements required much human effort. The riding machines gave some relief, and there was always the fun of adjusting levers and pressing pedals.

The horses were well trained for field work, but when plowing corn or cane, we made them wear muzzles to keep them from biting off the tops of the stalks. The horses also wore bridles with rear-view blinds so that they could not see any unusual activity behind them. The smarter ones soon learned to turn their heads to look back, and they kept their ears pricked up to listen for unusual noises.

Once while I was operating a two-span harrow, I saw a little rabbit nearby. I stopped the horses, laid down the reins, and ran after it. When the horses saw and heard this commotion, they started off full speed ahead across the twenty-acre field. The harrow bounced in leaps while I ran after the horses shouting "whoa, whoa, whoa," but they didn't mind me. When I saw the new harrow bounce and the horses run like wild zebras, I knew my farming career was coming to an end. I thought my father would reprimand me for wrecking the harrow and ruining a span of horses, but the animals had enough horse sense to stop by the field fence. Naturally, I kept the harrowing story between the horses, the fence post, and me.

Raising corn requires much hard work. The planting and plowing were easy enough because we used riding planters and cultivators, but chopping out weeds and harvesting the ears of corn by hand were not much fun. When harvesting the corn, we let the horses pull the wagon along, while three or four of us broke off the dry ears by hand and threw them into the wagon. When the horses got too far ahead of us, we yelled "whoa," and they stopped until we caught up and shouted "Get up, get up!"

To harvest corn-top fodder, we cut the tops after the tassels had shed their pollen on the silks and the ears were maturing. We walked along, grabbed the corn tops one at a time in our left arms, and cut them off above the ears. When we had an armful, we laid the bundle on the ground between the rows for drying. After these bundles were dry, we tied and stacked them. We made our own twine by cutting yucca bushes and ripping off the spiked blades. After cutting off the sharp thorns, we tied the blades together by two's, put them in bundles, and attached them to our belts, from which we pulled them out, one by one, as needed.

We tied the bundles early in the morning while the fodder was damp with dew. People told tales of farmers who picked up bundles containing rattlesnakes, and this frightened us. We usually kicked the fodder first to chase out any snakes before we tied it. Then we stacked the bundles and later hauled them to the haylofts in the barns or stacked them in round haystacks and oblong ricks.

We also grew some of the old-type grain sorghum with the typical shepherd-crook heads, and we called it milo maize. We harvested the heads of grain the same way we gathered corn, by letting the horses pull the wagon along the rows while we cut off the heads and pitched them into the wagon. It was an unpleasant task because the milo irritated our skin and caused itching and burning on our necks and arms. At home we dried the grain thoroughly and threshed it with cane poles.

We made hay from thickly growing sorghum cane, from Sudan grass, and from wheat and oats. We raked the dry, mowed hay into windrows and lifted it with pitchforks onto the wagon with the wide hay frame. Then we hauled it to the barns and unloaded it into the haylofts, or we stored it in haystacks or ricks. After hay balers came into use, we hauled the hay to the baler, stuffed it in by hand, and tied the bales with baling wire, while the horse-drawn plunger pressed it firmly.

Wild animals were also a part of ranching and farming, as they are to the present day. We boys hunted furbearing animals: raccoons, opossums, skunks, foxes, ringtails, and civet cats. We did our hunting at night with dogs, rifles, and lanterns. The dogs did the hunting, and we followed for the kill. Skunks with their pungent stink were a real problem. All the dogs kept a permanent skunk odor all winter long, and we the hunters also acquired a musky smell. Most of the furbearing animals were easy prey, but hunting raccoons was a spectacular sport; a big coon could give any dog or dogs a hard fight on the ground. In a pond or in the river, a raccoon usually won over a dog by holding the dog's head under water.

Some dogs put on a great show with their barking and baying while they were hot on the trail of an animal at night, and we added our part to the sound effects by blowing our horns, made from cow horns. A good hound dog or two could put on such hunting music that it alone was worth the effort of the hunt.

Game animals like deer were not as plentiful then as they are now. Predators, such as wildcats, wolves, and coyotes, killed off many of them, and there were no laws for the protection of wildlife. We shot deer occasionally for meat, but there was no hunting craze as we know it now. Some of our shooting was done to protect the field crops, but this did not do much good. Several times we sat up at night trying to guard our field peas and watermelons. On one occasion we fell asleep with loaded guns. Finally several deer appeared and snorted when they discovered us. Frank jumped up half-asleep, and his big shotgun went off with a boom.

During my ranch days all the buffalo or bison were gone; even during my father's childhood they were rare in our part of the country, so rare that children knew very little about them. When several of my father's brothers and sisters were children, they were sent out to the small pasture to bring home the milch cows, and there they spied a buffalo bull with the cows. They were so frightened that they ran home as fast as they could and reported, "The devil is with our cows."

We shot rabbits and squirrels to save our field crops and to control these animals' population explosion. Chicken hawks were always on our most-wanted list of criminals, but the hawks were as hard to shoot as crows, and they continued to thin out our chicks. There were always too many rats, mice, gophers, moles, lizards, and snakes, both useful and poisonous ones like rattlesnakes, water moccasins, and coral snakes. It is hard to distinguish a coral snake from a harmless king snake because their coloration is very similar, but the old jingle tells the difference: "Red and black, friend of Jack; / Red and yellow kills a fellow." Almost everybody is afraid of rattlesnakes, but few people are bitten by them, because rattlesnakes are stupid enough to give a warning by buzzing the rattlers on their tails, so their intended victims can jump out of striking distance. People reward the rattlers' considerate warning by clubbing them to death or shooting them with a shotgun. Boots are a good protection because most snake fangs cannot pierce good leather.

There is an apocryphal Mason County tale, though, about a fellow whose boots were pierced by snake fangs but whose skin was not broken. When he kicked the snake away, the fangs broke and remained stuck in the leather without his knowing it. When he put the boots on again later, the fangs pierced his skin, and he died without finding out what ailed him. Such wild stories prompt some people to bury a dead snake's head in a deep hole, so there will be no posthumous activity on the snake's part.

Little children and animals are more vulnerable than adults and are more likely to get bitten on their body or face. A snakebite on the foot, leg, or arm can be relieved by a properly adjusted tourniquet and by bleeding. Staying calm and seeing a doctor are imperative. Sometimes a dog, or even a small child, dies of a snakebite. An inscription on a tombstone at the grave of a ten-year-old girl in the Honey Creek Cemetery, in the hills west of New Braunfels, tells the sad story of such an accident. The inscription reads in German:

> Lucia Scheel (1891–1901)
> Des Morgens Schlangenbiss
> Macht Abends dir den Himmel gewiss.

(A morning bite by a snake
Brought heaven at night in its wake.)

The Hill Country, like most rural areas, has many insects, for instance, grasshoppers, mud daubers, wasps, scorpions, centipedes (we called them "santafees" in English), ants, various beetles, butterflies, moths, devil's horses, tarantulas, spiders, flies, bees, and mosquitoes. Most country kids have had their encounters with the stinging and biting varieties. We considered wasp fighting something of a sport. Armed with paddles, rocks, and sticks, we dared the wasps to do battle. When we found a large wasp nest in a tree or under the eaves of a house, we knocked the nest down with the rocks or sticks and then batted down the charging wasps. That is to say, we tried to bat them down. All too often the wasps stung us good and proper, and we suffered pains, swollen hands, and misshapen faces.

In our home and family life and in our agricultural enterprise, the major concern was work and more work; this was the essence of our being. A large family was raised so there would be many children to help, and the large family, in turn, made for even more work. It was an endless round of activities. Nevertheless, there was a time and place for other important concerns, namely the church and religion and the education of the children.

Sunday Meant Church

Oᴜʀ little community held several unusual records: first, for the large number of Methodist churches for its size—one southern and one northern Methodist Church—and second, for the high ratio of churches to stores—two to one. The abundance of churches indicates both a striking devotion to church work and an unfortunate divisiveness so often found in the various religious groups of the world. The southern branch of the German Methodist Church, to which my family belonged, stood on land donated by my grandfather, ten acres overlooking the Willow Creek from the west. It was built in 1890 and was designed by Richard Grosse, who lived for a while in Plehweville but later moved to Mason. Like so many structures in the German Hill Country, our Plehweville southern Methodist Church is a good specimen of rural, Texas-German stonemasonry. The architecture is German and Catholic-Lutheran, certainly not the humble typical American Methodist.

The church stands on an elevation and can be seen from afar, especially in the mornings from the eastern approach. The people wanted to build an impressive edifice, and they succeeded. The building, with its massive sandstone walls, has the traditional east-west orientation, and its steeple sits at the east end on the ridge of the steep roof. On this east end, there are two large, double, Gothic-arch doors, one for men and one for women. Six large, Gothic windows grace each of the side walls. People entering the church have the feeling of coming into a roomy sanctuary. Originally the inside walls were white lime plaster. The thing that always caught my eye was a modest inscription painted in gold on the wall above the pulpit. It proclaimed gently and appropriately, *Gott ist die Liebe* ("God is love"). The sign, with its symbol of the cross and crown, has disappeared, probably because nobody was able or willing to refurbish the old German lettering and the symbols when the interior of the church was painted. The floor, the slat pews, the pulpit, and the altar railing, as well as the pump organ, were all in natural wood.

The other German Methodist church in Plehweville, representing the northern branch, was smaller and less impressive than ours. It stood about a half-mile away, to the east across the Willow Creek. Of white-frame instead of stone construction, it more closely resembled an Anglo Methodist church house. The original division of the Methodist Church into a northern and a southern branch came about mostly as a result of the slavery question as early as 1844, but in Texas-German Methodism the break did not occur until the late 1860's, after the Civil War was over. Northern or Union sympathizers became active then, and about half the members of the German churches defected and organized northern Methodist congregations. Then in 1939 the two branches reunited to form the Methodist Church, a union appropriately symbolized locally when the frame church was moved across the creek and attached to the stone church as an activities building.

The peaceful sound of church bells ringing like an Angelus in small towns or across the countryside is unforgettable and reminiscent of rural solitude. The resonant "ding-dong, ding-dong, ding-dong" (German *bim-bam, bim-bam, bim-bam*) seems to say "come all, come all, come all!" This was everywhere the Sunday morning call to worship, but in German communities in Texas the bells were also tolled as evening bells (*Abendglocken*) on Saturday. I well remember how we could hear the church bells of the two Methodist churches at Plehweville ring at sunset on Saturday. This custom has been kept up in some small towns and rural communities of the Texas German Belt, so the *Abendglocken* can still be heard in some places. The big bell whose voice I heard as a child on the Willow Creek still tolls in its bell loft when the bellringer pulls the rope and sends out the "come-all" message in all directions.

I shall never forget my first secret visit to the steeple of the church. While we boys were in our vacation Bible school and catechism training, we explored the belfry during one noon hour. While the preacher ate his lunch in the parsonage, we climbed up the vertical ladder fastened to the east wall of the church and squeezed through a small manhole into the attic. Then we climbed still higher, up to the big bell, the *Glocke*, that we had heard ever since we were little children.

The bell rested in a strong frame where it could turn and swing back and forth. On one side was a large pulley wheel attached to the axle of the bell, and a rope was fastened to the wheel. When someone pulled the rope from the church floor, the bell swung to and fro and the heavy clapper struck first one side and then the other, causing the whole tower to vibrate with the mighty "gongs" and "clangs." I never had a call to preach, but while I was in Bible school and catechism training at the church, I had a great desire to ring the big bell someday. If being a preacher would entitle me to pull the long rope and toll the bell, I was almost persuaded to join the ministry when I grew up. After all, had I not memorized my Bible verses and the whole German catechism!

Sunday always meant church, and we attended regularly, health and weather permitting. We really had to be very sick or the weather had to be totally forbidding for us to stay at home on Sunday. This going to church meant a caravan of horses and vehicles, led by the two-span hack, with my father in the driver's seat on the right, my mother in the shotgun seat to the left, one or two tots with them in the front, and three or four half-grown children in the back, squeezed together tightly in the narrow seats or on the floor. A regular job for the little kids was to open and close the four gates on the road to the church.

The hack was followed by our buggy, which was drawn by one or two horses and carried another two or three people. The buggy was our sports car or convertible, similar to the Amish courting buggy, and the young folk showed off their style in it. In the early days, a two-wheel, two-passenger gig or several horseback riders followed the buggy. Because some people had to drive long distances, the church sessions were all-day affairs: morning worship, afternoon Sunday school, and another worship service. We carried several large lunch boxes full of food and dishes for our noonday meal and a number of bundles of corn-top fodder for the horses.

Each family had a camp on the church grounds. Ours was under some trees about one hundred yards north of the church. Here we had an ordinary, open-sided shed, with a permanent roof set on mesquite posts. Under the shed we put a long, homemade table and benches, where we ate our Sunday spread. Attached to the shed was a brush arbor, whose willow branches were laid on poles that rested on fork-topped mesquite posts. The arbor made good shade for sitting, and during camp meetings in summer it also served as a kitchen and general work area.

Each Sunday we drove to our camp, unhitched our herd of horses, and tied them to post-oak trees, where we gave them their fodder at noon. There was no work or play on Sunday; however, I was never able to figure out how this keeping the Sabbath holy jibed with all the work done by the women in preparing and serving the Sunday meals.

We carried not only food and fodder but also church and Sunday-school supplies: songbooks, Sunday school literature, little memory cards with Bible verses, and fans in summer. Most of the people carried their own thick songbooks, entitled *Gesangbuch der Bischöflichen Methodisten Kirche.* Measuring only 5¼ x 3¼ inches, they contained 780 songs and 12 benedictions and had 856 pages. They were bound in leather and were finished in beautiful gilt edging. The people who could read music carried hymnals with musical notes. All the people bought and carried their own songbooks because the church did not furnish hymnals.

We walked up the hill to the church and greeted our friends along the way or in front of the church with the usual, "Guten Morgen, wie geht's bei euch" ("Good morning, how are you all"), and we shook hands with everybody within reach. Then the men were separated from the women. The ladies entered the right (north) door and the men went in through the left (south) door. Even newlyweds parted before the portals of the church and sat in pews traditionally segregated by sex.

This separate seating was an old, unwritten rule. Women and bawling kids sat to the right, and the men and boys sat on the left side of the aisle. It was a great promotion for little boys when they crossed over to their father's realm. If sex segregation in the pews had started in our state, I would assume it was due to sex discrimination by the men, because in Texas the refreshing, summer breezes blow from the south, the men's side in the Hill Country, and the cold winter northers blow from the north, on the women's side.

After World War I the custom of separate pews for men and

women gradually broke down, and some of the younger couples crossed over the forbidden aisle. Most men and women, though, continued to sit separately up to World War II. When my father grew older in the 1930's and needed a little steadying support, he stayed by my mother's side and sat by her in the women's pew, but my mother would never have dared to cross over the aisle to the men's section. This seemed improper or immodest to her, and she would have been embarrassed to sit on the men's side.

As they entered the church, the men deposited their hats on the big box that contained the Christmas-tree ornaments and the camp-meeting tent. After entering the sanctuary, the people were quiet and devout. Occasionally the children whispered or giggled, but not for long, because the adults were in charge and kept order. When babies cried, their mothers took them outside.

After a short tolling of the bell by one of the lay leaders, the preacher stood up in the pulpit, made his introductory statement, and announced a song: "Wir beginnen unseren Gottesdienst im Namen des Vaters, des Sohnes und des Heiligen Geistes" ("We begin our divine service in the name of the Father, the Son, and the Holy Spirit"). "Lasst uns singen, Nummer 461." Then all the people arose, and while the pump organ played, they sang in loud voices, which almost raised the big roof:

> Mein Hirt ist der Herr,
> Dess bin ich so froh;
> Denn niemand, wie Er,
> Erbarmet sich so.
> Es kann ja den Seelen,
> Die Jesus regiert,
> Kein Gutes je fehlen,
> Der Herr ist mein Hirt.
> (*Gesangbuch,* 461)

This is an old German song, and it was sung to the tune of "O Worship the King," by Johann Michael Haydn. Since I am not familiar with any English translation, I will give my own:

> My shepherd, the Lord,
> Of this I'm so glad;
> No one, only He,
> Has mercy on me.
> And nothing is wanting

> For souls Jesus won;
> No good ever faileth;
> The Lord is my own.

The singing was powerful enough to make the church resound and reverberate. The people truly lifted up their voices to "make a joyful noise unto the Lord."

Then the preacher prayed while all the people turned around in the pews and knelt, propped their elbows on the benches, and covered their faces with their hands. It was as though God Himself had descended from great eternities to hear the prayer of thanks ("Wir danken Dir, lieber Gott . . . ") and the urgent pleas ("Wir bitten Dich, Herrgott, gib uns . . . "), and God needed no interpreter to translate the preacher's fervent German prayer.

Then the pastor stood up in the pulpit again, lifted the heavy, embossed, and gold-ornamented cover of the Bible, turned to the twenty-third Psalm, and read in clear and carefully enunciated German the Psalm of David, which begins as follows:

> Der Herr ist mein Hirte,
> Mir wird nichts mangeln.
> Er weidet mich auf einer grünen Aue
> Und führet mich zum frischen Wasser.

This was the Old Testament reading, and it was a lesson in elocution and literature as well as Bible lore. I can still hear the preacher, the Reverend A. R. Vetter, roll the resonant *r* sounds in *Herr, Hirte,* and *mir,* and bring out the effective *h* alliteration in *Herr, Hirte,* and *Haus,* the *m* in *mein, mir, mangeln, mich,* and *meine,* the *l* in *Leben lang,* the *st* in *Stecken und Stab,* or the rich *U-Umlaut* in words like *grünen, führet, fürchte,* and *Unglück.*

If the Twenty-third Psalm is properly read, there is really no need for a sermon, but at this point we were just beginning. Now the preacher called upon some lay member to pray. This was done without warning, and all the pillars of the church were ready to respond to the pastor's call. It was an honor to be called on to pray, and most of the men got their turn sooner or later. These prayers drew the congregation into full participation.

After the layman's prayer, the pastor said, "Lasst uns singen! Nummer 505." With a view to the New Testament the congregation sang the familiar song "Voran, voran mit Jesu" ("Stand Up, Stand Up for Jesus"). Then the minister read the New Testament lesson from the Sermon on the Mount in the sixth chapter of Matthew, verses 25–34:

> Darum sage ich euch sorget nicht für euer Leben,
> was ihr essen und trinken werdet; auch nicht für
> euren Leib, was ihr anziehen werdet. Ist nicht das
> Leben mehr denn die Speise, und der Leib mehr denn
> die Kleidung?

> (Therefore I say unto you, Take no thought for your
> life, what ye shall eat, or what ye shall drink; nor
> yet for your body, what ye shall put on. Is not the life
> more than meat, and the body than raiment?)

Then followed the receiving of the offering. The organist, someone like Minnie or Lydia Jordan or Ella Eckert, played "Segensströme" ("Showers of Blessing"), and the people sang the chorus by heart:

> Ströme, Ströme voll Segen,
> Tropfen genügen uns nicht;
> Sende uns gnädige Regen,
> Wie es dein Wort uns verspricht.
> (*Die Kleine Palme*, 125)

> (Showers, showers of blessing,
> Showers of blessing we need:
> Mercy drops round us are falling,
> But for the showers we plead.)
> (*Church Hymns and
> Gospel Songs*, 305)

Several ushers fetched their Stetson hats and passed them along, while the congregation dropped in their offering. Not even the coins made any noise as they landed on the soft felt.

Then the pastor delivered his well-prepared sermon. He urged the people to forget their earthly possessions and their concern over the everyday affairs of life and to think with him on eternal things. This they tried to do, but it is hard to lay aside the cares of life when you are worried over the prospects of a drought and caring for herds of cattle. And how could the women lay aside their household cares and worries over food and raiment! Nevertheless, through the preacher's plea, they were encouraged, and at least for the time being life took on a new meaning.

After the sermon came another song, *Nummer 591*, and the singing woke up those who had dozed off during the sermon:

> Auf, denn die Nacht wird kommen,
> Auf, mit dem jungen Tag!
> Wirket am frühen Morgen,
> Eh's zu spät sein mag.
> (*Gesangbuch*, 591)

> (Work, for the night is coming,
> Work through the morning hours;
> Work while the dew is sparkling,
> Work 'mid springing flow'rs.)
> (*The New Cokesbury Hymnal*, 201)

This song made good sense to the people. They were up and at it all the time anyway, from early morning until late at night, and work was the meaning of their lives.

Then came another prayer, and at the close of the service the people stood up and sang:

> Nimm, Jesu, meine Hände
> Und führe mich,
> Bis an mein selig Ende
> Und ewiglich!
> Ich kann allein nicht gehen,
> Nicht einen Schritt;
> Wo Du wirst geh'n und stehen,
> Da nimm mich mit!
> (*Gesangbuch*, 196)

> (O take my hand, dear Father,
> And lead thou me,
> Till at my journey's ending
> I dwell with thee.
> Alone I cannot wander
> One single day,
> So do thou guide my footsteps
> On life's rough way.)
> (Translated by H. Brueckner in the Lutheran *Service Book and Hymnal*, 292)

Daniel and Emilie Jordan, about 1900. Father's characteristic pose was with his head held high, looking the world straight in the eye. Mother could be stern when the occasion demanded, but she was also loving and kind.

Father was a *Mädchenvater* (a "father of girls") in the early days. Five of his first six children, pictured here about 1895, were girls. *Standing, left to right:* Hulda, Anna, Ida, Dina. *Sitting:* Dan and Olga.

The whole Jordan family journeyed to Mason to give a rural-Gothic pose, about 1908. *Top, left to right:* Ida, John Schuessler, Anna, and Dan. *Middle:* Olga and Frank. *Front:* Gilbert, Hulda, Daniel (Father), Emily (in Mother's lap), Emilie (Mother), Dina, and Milton.

Home on the Willow Creek, the Daniel Jordan ranch home near Plehwe-ville (Art), about 1920.

Bringing in the melons for the *Wassermelonenschmier* ("watermelon spread"), 1924.

The author by the old dug well at the home on the Willow Creek, 1975.
(Photo by Terry G. Jordan)

The author with twin pet lambs, 1914.

Emil Hoerster and Daniel Jordan, keeping an eye on their cattle while eating lunch by the wagon, Blue Mountain Ranch, about 1910. (Photo by Fred Bickenbach)

Old rock fence, post-and-rail fence, slat gates, and chute in the cowpens at the Standke place, 1975. (Photo by Terry G. Jordan)

Picket fences like this one were built to enclose cowpens. Hoerster Ranch in the Blue Mountains in Mason County, 1975. Terry Jordan provides the scale for the height of the fence.

Two horseback riders ready to ride to church, about 1912. Others will follow in the hack and buggy in the background. (Photo courtesy of Mrs. Edwin Donop, née Hulda Jordan)

Group of young people with their hacks, about 1912. (Photo courtesy of Mrs. Edwin Donop, née Hulda Jordan, *fourth from left*)

The Jordan churchyard pavilion and brush arbor, fallen into disrepair after camp meetings were discontinued.

The Art Methodist Church, 1970, formerly called the Upper Willow Creek M.E. Church, South, at Plehweville, built in 1890 on land donated by Ernst Jordan.

A group of women beside the big circus tent used for camp meetings in the Ernst Jordan pecan bottoms, during the 1880's. (Photo from the Daniel Jordan collection, courtesy of Mrs. Edwin Donop)

Confirmation class of the Plehweville M.E. Church, South, about 1912, the Reverend H. Jordan, pastor. (Photo courtesy of Mrs. W. O. Schulze, née Olga Jordan, *fourth from left, front row*)

Vera Jordan by a typical rock fence on the Mason-Fredericksburg highway, 1926.

Plehweville School, District 6, Mason County, 1910–1911 school year. The author is second from left, first row standing.

Deutsches

Erstes Lesebuch

Für amerikanische Schulen.

von

W. H. Weick und C. Grebner.

New York ∴ Cincinnati ∴ Chicago
American Book Company.

Title page of *Deutsches Erstes Lesebuch für amerikanische Schulen* (New York, 1886). This book and others in the same series were widely used for German classes in the bilingual elementary schools before World War I.

Christmas card showing a Santa Claus in a blue suit and with a basket of toys, about 1910.

A sturdy German-Texas sandstone house, the old Georg Philip Eckert home near Hilda in Mason County, built in 1870. (Photo courtesy of Mrs. Frank Jordan, née Ella Eckert)

A Victorian showplace in Mason, Texas, is the Reynolds-Seaquist home, built of sandstone and ornamented with porches, towers, railings, and gables. The house has seventeen rooms. (Photo, 1974)

The Schmidt Blacksmith Shop that stood on the east side of the Mason square. (Photo courtesy of Sterling [Pete] Schmidt)

Interior view of the old Commercial Bank in Mason, Texas. (Photo courtesy of Mrs. Sam Eckert, née Ethyl Lehmberg)

Mason County Courthouse in the 1930's. (Photo courtesy of University of Texas Library)

Scene on the Mason square, probably a Confederate reunion between 1915 and 1920. This is the transition time from horse-drawn vehicles to automobiles. (From a postcard, courtesy of Mrs. F. P. Alexander)

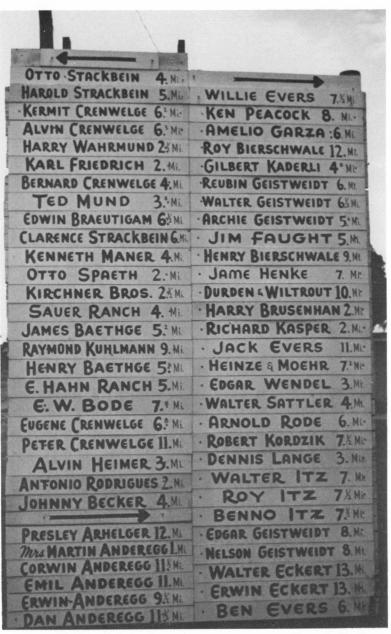

Rural road signboard at Doss, between Mason and Fredericksburg, showing predominance of German family names, 1975.

Then the pastor dismissed his flock with a short benediction:

> Die Gnade unsers Herrn Jesu Christi,
> Und die Liebe Gottes,
> Und die Gemeinschaft des heiligen Geistes
> Sei mit uns Allen. Amen!
>
> (*Gesangbuch*, 807)

> (The grace of the Lord Jesus Christ
> And the love of God
> And the fellowship of the Holy Spirit
> Be with you all. Amen.)
>
> (*The Methodist Hymnal*, 763)

Because of the anti-German feeling and prejudice accompanying World War I, English worship services began to replace the German after 1917. The transition was a difficult change and a traumatic experience, especially for the elderly people, and most of all for elderly women. Young people had learned their English well in school, and most men had become accustomed to it through their association with English-speaking ranchmen and businessmen. For them the changeover was much easier than for the German-Texas *Hausfrau*. Nevertheless, it was something of a shock for all the German-speaking people to hear the Lord God speak in English through the King James translation of the Bible in place of the familiar Martin Luther version. And it was anything but a religious experience to hear some old German pastor shift to a heavily German-accented English sermon or scripture reading.

It is one thing to learn to speak and understand a new language, but it is something else again to preach and pray in it. The German-oriented preachers made a brave attempt to adjust to English, and some became surprisingly proficient. This was especially true of the Reverend F. W. Radetzky, who could deliver a bilingual sermon, translating every German sentence into English. He could also preach an eloquent German sermon and immediately shift to English and deliver the same sermon verbatim in English. The Reverend Robert Moerner, who was something of a schoolmaster anyway, could also do well in this sort of service.

The hardest adjustment of all was to learn to pray in a second language. That is almost as difficult as learning to dream in a foreign tongue. There are many crystallized phrases in the prayers, and the people's ears are attuned to them. Such things cannot be learned; they must be absorbed by frequent contact with other speakers of the language.

If the shift from German to English in prayers was hard for the preachers, it was completely out of the question for many of the ordinary church members. No matter how much they might have said, "Lord, teach us how to pray in English," it did no good at all, because the Lord continued to speak in German to the people, and they spoke in German to Him. As a result of the inability of some of the older, most loyal church members to learn to pray in English, an interesting bilingual service developed. When the English services became more or less necessary, the preachers performed as best they could in the pulpit, but when they called on members to pray, the prayers were in German. I can no more imagine either one of my parents praying in English than I can envision them as astronauts flying to the moon. They and some of the people of their age-group learned perhaps how to reel off the Lord's Prayer, but that is as far as their English communication with God ever went.

The transition from German to English church songs was a simple matter compared with the change in sermons and prayers. From the very beginning, the Methodists were singers, originally under the leadership of the Wesleys and Whitefield in England. Umphrey Lee in his book on John Wesley says that "the new movement was a singing movement." The German Methodists in America not only continued the English predilection for singable songs but added the German love of singing, and they made hundreds of translations of English songs.

Many of the songs in the German Methodist Hymnal were translations from the English Methodist Hymnal. Here are a few of the songs that were most familiar to us, presented with their English and German titles: "Lord Jesus, I Love Thee" ("Herr Jesus, dich lieb ich"), "He Leadeth Me!" ("Er führet mich"), "Jesus, Lover of My Soul" ("Jesus, Heiland meiner Seele"). All the above-listed songs were sung to the same tune in the two languages, except the last one, which was known to us in English in the tune by S. B. Marsh and in German in the tunes by Ithamar Conkey and L. Mason. Incidentally, Schwarz's German version of the lyrics avoids the sentimental word *lover* used by Charles Wesley, substituting *savior*, so it reads: "Jesus, Savior of my Soul." There are also a number of German songs in the English Methodist hymnal which we already knew in German and which we rediscovered as dear old friends. Among these are: "Ein' feste Burg ist unser Gott" ("A Mighty Fortress Is Our God"), "Nun danket alle Gott" ("Now Thank We All Our God"), "Stille Nacht, heilige Nacht" ("Silent Night, Holy Night"), and "Wer nur den lieben Gott lässt walten" ("If Thou but Suffer God to Guide Thee").

The tradition of singing German church songs has continued to the present day, and there has been a renewal of interest in the old hymns. After World War II, and ever since 1950, annual songfests have been held in the former German churches; hundreds of people come, and all join in the singing. This interest has continued to grow, and in 1975 the twenty-fifth anniversary of the songfests was celebrated in the Art Church as a local contribution to the national Bicentennial celebration. Even younger people are discovering or rediscovering their ethnic heritage in these song festivals.

Sunday school was at first mostly for the children and younger people, but adult classes also became very active. The sessions opened with a general program of singing, reading, prayer, and an exhortation by the Sunday school superintendent. The songs were mostly lively and appealing to young people. The little children were taught to sing several songs in German. Our favorite was "Gott ist die Liebe; Lässt mich erlösen" ("God is All Loving; He Would Redeem Me"). Another charming song with youth appeal was "Wir sind kleine Schnitter," which appears in *Die Kleine Palme* (page 9). The song reads in my translation as follows:

> We are little reapers,
> Working hard with might;
> On the spreading grainfields
> Gleams the harvest white.
> Storm and rain and downpours
> Do not overwhelm;
> We are gath'ring sheaves here
> For the heavenly realm.
>
> *Refrain*
> Working, working is the reaper's fate;

Working, working; our reward is great.
(*Repeat last four lines of the stanza.*)

Among the English favorites for children were "Jesus Wants Me for a Sunbeam," "Bringing in the Sheaves," and "Jesus Loves Me, This I Know."

The young people were fond of the cheerful German song "Immer fröhlich" ("Always Joyful") from *Lobe den Herrn* (page 14). My translation reads:

Let our hearts be always joyful
And be filled with thanks and cheer.
For our Father who's in heaven
Calls us all his children, dear.

Refrain
Always joyful, always joyful,
Sunshine every day we see.
Full of beauty is life's pathway always,
Joyful may we ever be.

English favorites that were often sung in Sunday school are "Count Your Blessings," "I Love to Tell the Story," "Blessed Assurance," and dozens of others.

After the introductory program, the classes met separately in groups at various places all over the sanctuary. There was much talking, and the groups disturbed each other to some extent, but we did not let this stop us. The little children recited short Bible verses from flower-adorned cards that we called tickets. After a child had memorized and recited five, ten, or fifteen such verses, he received a prize of a larger card with pretty flowers and a Bible verse.

After Sunday school came another worship service similar to the one in the morning. Occasionally a young people's service, such as the Epworth League or a song practice, took the place of the afternoon session. Then followed much visiting with friends and relatives before the people returned to their homes. On certain Sundays of the month, when they had not had them earlier in the day, the young people had evening Epworth League services and occasionally a song practice. These activities were largely in the hands of youth groups and they offered good leadership training. Dating also played a role in these gatherings. The boys took this opportunity to come by for their girl friends and take them back home in their courting buggies. From 1915 on, they used the family cars.

Much of the program centered around singing songs. We used special songbooks like *Die Kleine Palme* ("The Little Palmtree"), *Lobe den Herrn* ("Praise the Lord"), and *Church Hymns and Gospel Songs*. We sang some German songs, but most of them were English, such as "Oh, There Will Be Glory," "Shall We Gather at the River," and "Blessed Assurance" ("Süsse Gewissheit"). Several of the songs were known to us equally well in English and in German, like the last one mentioned above. We really let the chorus ring out:

> This is my story, this is my song,
> Praising my Savior all the day long.
> (*Methodist Hymnal*, 224)

> Dies ist mein Lied, ich sing' es so gern.
> Täglich und stündlich preis' ich den Herrn.
> (*Die Kleine Palme*, 21)

The German Methodists' custom of holding a catechism school showed the influence of the German Evangelical, Lutheran, and Catholic churches, to which almost all the original settlers had belonged at one time. Although in the early days of the Anglo Methodist Church catechisms were published and used, during my days there was little of this left in the Anglo churches, and this was a major difference between the German and Anglo Methodists in Texas. When the children were twelve to sixteen years old, they entered this Bible school. In our community it was a vacation or summer school, and it lasted from four to six weeks. We took along our lunches and made a day of it each time.

The school was conducted by the pastor, and the children memorized Bible passages, church songs, and the answers to the questions in the catechism booklets. Some of the answers were incomprehensible to thirteen-year-old children, but we memorized them anyway, as if they had been dictated by the Holy Ghost. On Confirmation Sunday the pupils were examined by the preacher in the presence of the whole congregation. On this Sunday there was only a short sermon or none at all because the examination took up most of the time. The children all received certificates of recognition and Bibles presented and signed by the minister. My Bible is printed on thin India paper and bound in black leather. The gold lettering in front reads *Die Heilige Schrift*, and the Bible has a red gilt edge with rounded corners.

My certificate of recognition, written in German, named the date and place of my examination and was "certified with cordial good wishes by W. D. Wiemers, Pastor". The certificate is adorned with flowers, at the top is a pulpit with an open Bible, and in the background landscape stands a country church. Mottoes appear at four places, and the most prominent one is *Gottes Furcht ist aller Weisheit Anfang* ("The fear of God is the beginning of all wisdom").

On confirmation day the catechism class was received into membership of the church, and we partook of the Lord's Supper for the first time. We walked to the altar, knelt down, and the preacher, assisted by a local preacher or exhorter, passed along pieces of homemade bread and the large communion cup. While the preachers administered the bread and wine, they mumbled words like "Take and eat this in remembrance that Christ died for thee . . . The blood, which was shed for thee, preserve thy soul and body . . . ," all this in German. Then came a verse of scripture, a poem, the chorus of a song, and the pastor said something like "Gottes Segen begleite euch" ("May the blessings of God go with you"). We returned to our seats while others came to the altar. I think the common communion cup was used until the flu epidemic of 1918. Then the little individual cups were introduced, and all you got was a tiny sip.

We were glad the testing and the ceremony were over. The boys had been uncomfortable in new suits with long pants and in stiff new shirts and shoes, and the girls had suffered in new, starched, white dresses and large, decorated hats. We all looked strange to each other, and our parents must have felt proud and sad at the same time to see their children suddenly almost grown and dressed like adults.

There was much fanning and wiping of brows on this hot July day. I still remember the old palm-leaf fans that the men swished back and forth and the dainty Japanese folding fans the ladies waved to and fro with a gentle touch. We also had cardboard fans with wooden handles stapled on and with advertisements by the Mason merchants who gave them away. On the front were pictures of ladies, horses, and scenes. These cardboard fans were often distributed for camp meetings, where the advertisements by the stores and the funeral parlors reached many potential customers. These fans were not as appropriate for our Confirmation Sunday as the palm-leaf and Japanese folding fans. I think some of the women carried dainty, white handkerchiefs in their hymnals on this day.

The influence of the church carried over into our home life. Every morning and evening we had family devotionals, called *Andacht* in German. These services consisted of reading selections from the Bible and a prayer, and they were an unfailing routine in our home. After the Bible reading, we turned around at our chairs or benches, knelt down, placed our elbows on our chairs, and held our heads in our hands.

Prayers played a big role in our lives. We memorized the children's prayers in German and spoke them as we knelt by our beds before going to sleep. Here is one of these little prayers:

> Ich bin klein,
> Mein Herz mach' rein;
> Soll niemand drin wohnen,
> Als Jesus allein.

> (I am small,
> My heart make pure;
> None shall there dwell,
> But Jesus, for sure.)

Another beginner's prayer was:

> Lieber Gott, mach' mich fromm,
> Dass ich zu Dir in'n Himmel komm!

> (Dear God, let me pious be,
> That I may get to heaven with Thee.)

As we grew a little older, we memorized the following German favorite by Luise Hensel, which is similar to the English "Now I lay me down to sleep, I pray the Lord my soul to keep." It has some additional verses, but here are the most frequently used lines:

> Müde bin ich, geh' zur Ruh',
> Schliesse meine Äuglein zu;
> Vater, lass die Augen Dein
> Über meinem Bette sein.
> Hab' ich Unrecht heut' getan,
> Sieh's, mein lieber Gott, nicht an!

(Tired am I, go to bed,
Close my eyes, lay down my head;
Father, let the eyes of Thine
O'er my resting place incline.
If I've done some wrong today,
Take, dear Lord, my guilt away.)

There is usually some joker in every community who thinks up parodies, even on serious matters like prayers. Here is a prize takeoff on the first children's prayer quoted above:

Ich bin klein,
Mein Magen ist gross;
Soll nichts hinein,
Als Speck und Soss'.

(I am small
My stomach is big;
Nothing shall get in,
But gravy and pig. [literally, bacon])

Prayer meetings were held in the homes of the church members, usually on Tuesday or Wednesday afternoons, and whole families came. The preacher was in charge. After reading a passage from the Bible, he made brief comments. Then the prayers started, and a song followed every two German prayers. One of the favorite songs was "What a Friend We Have in Jesus," sung in German:

Welch ein treuer Freund ist Jesus,
Der da immer hilft so gern!
Welch ein Vorrecht ist's zu bringen
Alles in Gebet zum Herrn!
(*Gesangbuch*, 429; English in
The Methodist Hymnal, 275).

All of the prayers were in German, and most were spoken voluntarily. Everybody had his turn, but occasionally the preacher called on young people and timid members, who responded sometimes with unexpected fervency, but sometimes in almost inaudible mumbling.

After the prayer session, refreshments were served or, better said, an afternoon dinner was served, consisting of several kinds of homemade cheese, cured sausage, bread and butter, jelly and preserves, layer cake, coffee cake, and, of course, coffee. These big feasts were the undoing of the home prayer meetings. Some of the good ladies got tired of feeding a whole congregation of hungry souls. The prayer meetings shifted to the church, and all the people went home hungry. That was good for neither the body nor the soul, so the prayer-meeting time was reset for the evening, after supper.

Summer camp meetings were as typical of the German as of the Anglo Methodist church. Although conversion to Methodism was at first a major adjustment for some of the German Texans, once converted they adapted themselves quickly to the American revival technique and the brush-arbor camping. Three of my grandparents had been Protestants before they came to Texas, and for them the conversion to Methodism was not as difficult as it was for my grandfather Anton Willmann. He was first attracted by the excitement of a German Methodist meeting, but since he was a Catholic, he did not dare attend. He only listened to the proceeding from the concealment of some bushes. Finally he ventured out from his hiding place and accepted Methodism, and he became a true Wesleyan zealot. At one camp meeting he was swept along so powerfully by the Methodist fervor that he forgot about his pregnant wife Christina, who had stayed at home. When he finally returned to the house, the time was near that Christina should be delivered, and she was upset that he had been absent at so critical an hour. But when he told her that he had helped convert his older children to Methodism, she gladly forgave him for staying so long, and soon she presented him with yet another child to be converted. This birth was nothing unusual for Anton; he fathered twenty children in all, seven by his first wife and thirteen by Christina, his second.

The German settlers living on isolated ranches were starved for social contacts like those they had had in Fredericksburg and in the German villages. The camp meetings provided this much-needed association with relatives and friends, as well as the religious communication. Especially the young people and the children enjoyed the camping experience and playing and talking together.

The German settlers brought the Methodist camp meetings to Mason County in the 1860's. The meetings were at first held under brush arbors on the south side of the Llano River. Then beginning in 1876 these early revivals were held under circus tents in the pecan bottoms on the east bank of the Willow Creek on my grandfather's place. After the turn of the century, open-sided tabernacles with shingle or metal roofs were built near the churches; these are still in use for summer revivals. Most of the families used pavilions and large brush arbors, and they brought tents to be used in addition to covered wagons for sleeping quarters.

The family camping facilities were semipermanent and were also used for day camping each Sunday, as was mentioned above. The brush arbors had to be renovated every few years by adding new poles and fresh willow branches and twigs, and extensive preparations were made each year for the camp-out. Wagonloads of equipment and supplies—tents, beds, bedding, cots, stoves, chairs, benches, tables, cooking utensils, dishes, food, clothes, horse feed, and fodder —had to be hauled to the camps.

Providing almost a week's worth of food for a large family as well as for visitors and preachers required much work. Enough bread was baked at home to last the entire time of the camp meeting, and some canned food and sausage were carried along, ready to serve. But since great quantities of fresh beef had to be supplied and cooked, local butchers brought the beef to the camps and sold it to the people.

A typical camp-meeting day began with a hearty breakfast at the various family camps. The large staff of preachers, who came from all the surrounding churches and camped in special tents or in the church building, had their meals with the people. They often led the devotionals after breakfast. There were scripture readings and prayers, the same as in the home devotionals, and church songs. It was an inspiring experience to hear the different families sing at their camps, scattered all over the church grounds. I can still hear some of these songs resound. One such song was "Ich weiss einen Strom, dessen herrliche Flut" (*Gesangbuch*, 289), which reads in my translation as follows:

> I know a river's glorious stream
> Flows wondrously still through the land;
> Yet it shines and glows in a fiery gleam.
> Who knows of this water's strand?
>
> *Refrain*
> Oh my soul, I ask thee to come,
> And seek out this glorious stream;

Its water flows freely and strong;
Believe that it flows to redeem.

At another family camp the people were singing "Süsse Gewiss-heit" ("Blessed Assurance"), while a third group sang:

Niemals fürchtet euch, ein Wort zu reden
Für den Heiland, euren Herrn.
                    (*Gesangbuch*, 469)

(Never fear to speak a word for Jesus,
For your Savior, for your Lord.)

Then farther down the hillside a fourth family began to sing:

Lasst mich geh'n, lasst mich geh'n,
Dass ich Jesum möge seh'n.
                    (*Gesangbuch*, 571)

(Let me go, let me go,
That my Jesus I may know.)

And so it went from camp to camp, one family after another started to sing, and sometimes they sang simultaneously. Thus the people's songs rang out among the trees, the tents, and the wagons. Occasionally a horse neighed, a neighbor's dog barked somewhere, or somebody called out a cheerful "Guten Morgen." The whole churchyard was fragrant from wood campfires, fried bacon, sausage, and boiling coffee.

After breakfast and the morning devotionals, the people prepared for the day's activities. The women took their turns at the little outhouses, and the men withdrew to the Willow Creek or behind trees and rock fences. Dishes were washed under the brush arbors, beds were straightened up in the tents and in the covered wagons, and food was prepared for the day. Then everybody got dressed for the morning church services held under the big circus tent.

The morning and afternoon services resembled regular church sessions, with perhaps more of a revival spirit than was heard in the regular Sunday services. A festive air touched all the worshipers. With a half-dozen preachers present and all the people gathered together, a tremendous enthusiasm took hold of the congregation. While the cicadas (some people called a cicada a *Schreihals* in German, "a screamer") chirped and screamed in the oak trees, the preachers took turns at praying and preaching. Everyone felt that this service was something special, but the climax of each day was the evening revival meeting.

In the late afternoon or immediately after supper, many small groups gathered together to pray for abundant blessings at the evening services. And then after supper the people assembled in the big tent. Coal-oil lamps hanging on posts under the tent furnished the light. These were old-fashioned torches that burned open flames, raised a big stench, and produced unwanted heat. Fortunately there was often a strong south breeze that blew away the odors and heat, but the wind also caused the scalloped edges of the tent to make a flapping noise. However, once the singing, praying, and preaching started, nobody heard the flapping anymore.

Hope for success and encouragement were found in scripture and song assuring the people of God's promises. One number often sung, an encouraging theme song, was "Wasserströme will ich giessen" (*Gesangbuch*, 660). Translated into English, the song says:

> "Streams of water I'll be pouring,"
> Says the Lord, "on desert land;
> Cooling springs will soon be flowing
> O'er the desert's burning sand.
> Where the trav'lers now are pining,
> Will God's garden soon be shining."

I could never accept the doctrine of original sin, but I, like all the others, responded at some time or other to the preachers' pleading and the appeal of songs like "So wie ich bin" ("Just as I Am") and "Gehe nicht vorbei, O Heiland" ("Pass Me Not, O Gentle Savior").

We did not have a "sawdust trail"; we did not even have any sawdust in our country of scrubby oaks, cedars, and mesquites, but we did have a Willow-Creek gravel path, which led to the "mourners' bench." The preachers hovered over the penitents and urged them to confess all their sins and then rejoiced over "the lamb that was lost and has been found."

At the close of the last service on Sunday night a beautiful ceremony was held. All the people rose, marched out of the tent or tabernacle, and formed a large double circle. Then, while marching in opposite directions, they shook hands and sang "Gott mit euch, bis wir uns wiederseh'n" (*Gesangbuch*, 772):

> God be with you till we meet again;
> By his counsels guide, uphold you,
> With his sheep securely fold you:
> God be with you till we meet again.
> (*The Methodist Hymnal*, 539)

In the early German camp meetings, everybody sang the song in German, but later some sang it in English and some, in German. That did not matter at all, because either way the tune was the familiar one by W. G. Tomer, including the chorus, which has been deleted in recent editions of the *Methodist Hymnal*. The people went home spiritually renewed and mentally refreshed.

Funeral services were sad, heart-rending occasions. After the death watch or vigil came a short service in the home of the deceased and a slow funeral procession to the church. When my sister Dina died, I rode in the procession with Brother Radetzky in his buggy. He tried to console me by assuring me that now I had a sister in heaven, whom I would meet some day in glory. This was a well-meant consolation, but it did not impress me very much because I missed her too much here below.

A full funeral service with a long sermon followed in the church. The first song was "Heimatland, Heimatland, O wie schön bist du" ("Heavenly Home, Heavenly Home, Oh How Fair and Blest"). It makes me sad every time I hear it now or think of it. Then came the song that always moves me deeply and depresses me because of its association with Dina's funeral:

> In dem Himmel ist's wunderschön,
> O, wie gerne möcht' ich dort steh'n,
> Wo statt Kampf, Schmerz und Hohn
> Meiner wartet die Kron',
> Wo ich darf meinen Heiland seh'n.
> (*Gesangbuch*, 571)

> (In heaven it's wondrously fair,
> O, I yearn to be lifted there;
> Instead of strife, pain, and scorn,
> A crown will adorn,
> And I'll see my dear Savior up there.)

Throughout the long service and sermon the open coffin stood in front of the altar in full view of the congregation. All the people walked past and viewed the body for the last time. This was a trying, tear-filled ceremony, and it left us exhausted and totally depressed.

The third and final part of the funeral was the graveside service. The pallbearers carried the coffin to the hack in which it had been brought to the church, and while the slow "gongs" of the funeral bell sounded in the belfry, the procession moved to the open grave. After scripture readings, prayers, and a song, Brother Radetzky took a shovel of soil and poured three portions of it into the open grave, while he spoke these words, "Erde zu Erde, Asche zu Asche, Staub zu Staub." The graveyard dirt, symbolizing the traditional earth, ashes, and dust, rumbled as it hit the wooden casket box, and we cringed and wept while the heavy earth fell down from the preacher's shovel. Then we stayed by the graveside while strong young men filled the grave and shaped the mound on top and put on the flowers. Months later my mother put shells on the grave. This is an old pre-Christian custom, less common now than some fifty years ago, and whose meaning my mother did not even know. In addition to her name, dates of birth and death, and a Biblical inscription or motto, there is not much special information carved on Dina's stone, such as is found in some German Catholic cemeteries where gravestones often list the birthplace, especially if the person was foreign-born.

On the tombstone of my grandparents, Ernst and Lisette Jordan, there are two special inscriptions in German: *Durch Kreuz zur Krone* ("By way of the cross to the crown") and *Selig sind die Toten, die im Herrn sterben. Off.* 14:13 ("Blessed are the dead which die in the Lord. Rev. 14:13"). There are several other German inscriptions, such as this one for Dessie Kothmann, 1903–1905: "*In Christum gibt's ein Auferstehen, / Da werden wir uns wiedersehen*" ("In Christ we will arise again; / Then we will all meet again"). One inscription, on the gravestone of Charles and Sophie Kothmann, is even carved in the old German or Gothic letters and simply states, *Auf wiedersehen*.

An interesting custom has developed in the German-Texas Hill Country and other rural areas. Deaths and funerals are announced publicly by posting black-bordered notices listing the name of the deceased and the time and place of the funeral. These printed notices appear at the entrances of the main stores in the towns.

In the early days most families had private graveyards near their homes, but after 1900 the rural church cemeteries took their place. Nevertheless, many of the old family cemeteries still remain, and in the German Belt they are frequently surrounded by stone walls. Two good examples of such walled plots are the Kothmann and Jordan cemeteries at Art. One of the finest private stone-wall cemeteries is that of John O. Meusebach near Cherry Spring, between Mason and Fredericksburg.

Funerals are well attended in the German-Texas Hill Country, with people coming by the hundreds from far and near. The women of the church prepare and serve dinner to the immediate family and all out-of-town relatives. This custom has developed in the last fifty years or more, and it relieves the immediate family of much worry and care. These are not funeral feasts in the European peasant tradition, but rather modest meals for the bereaved.

Our little community was so strongly religious that our whole lives revolved around the church and its activities. Not only did we attend divine services every Sunday, go to camp meeting once each year, and participate in home prayer meetings each week, but our entire daily lives were influenced by the church's teachings and practices. We had home devotionals twice each day, table prayers or blessings before each meal, and bedtime prayers every night. Even in our music and singing we used primarily church and Sunday-school hymns and songs. We sang these songs in groups around the pump organ in the parlor or while riding horseback or in hacks and buggies, and we sang while doing our ranch and farm work, even when working alone. The church was everywhere: in weddings, christenings, funerals, holidays, in our readings, in Bible and catechism schools, in our sayings and proverbs. Along with our work ethic, discussed earlier, and education, to be considered next, the church was a powerful influence in our lives.

6

The Little
Brown Schoolhouse

A one-room, sandstone school standing near the east bank of the Willow Creek was the place where I received my first formal schooling. My father and his brothers and sisters had attended this school in the 1850's, 1860's, and 1870's, when it was still housed in a log cabin, built in 1858 on land donated by my pioneer paternal grandfather. The log building served at first as both the school and the southern Methodist Church. One of the first teachers was Otto von Donop, who had studied at the prestigious University of Berlin. Noblemen and scholars like von Donop had earlier (in 1847) established utopian settlements in Texas, one at Bettina on the Llano River between Castell and Llano and the other at Sisterdale on the Guadalupe between San Antonio and Fredericksburg. The noblemen soon dropped the "von-ny" business and became plain American citizens with the egalitarian title of "Mister." After the original log schoolhouse was burned down by a gang of cattle rustlers during the Hoodoo War in Mason County in the 1870's, the brown-stone building, where I went to school from 1910 to 1919, replaced it.

It is surprising how successful the educational results were, considering the fact that sometimes one teacher had from forty to sixty pupils in one room. There were some advantages to be gained from having several grades in the same room. The younger children learned a few things from the more advanced classes by listening to their recitations, and the nonlearners in the upper grades heard the work of the lower grades repeated year after year. In this way they might learn in the fifth grade what they were supposed to have learned in the first and second.

We had the *Golden Song Books* and we sang the old familiar songs like "My Country 'Tis of Thee," "Columbia, the Gem of the Ocean," "We're Tenting on the Old Campground," "Dixie," "Old Black Joe," "Long, Long Ago," and "Flow Gently, Sweet Afton."

Many a long forgotten verse comes back to me, and I hear myself and my schoolmates sing "Oh, My Darling Nellie Gray" and "My Bonnie Lies over the Ocean." We also sang some German songs like "Die Lorelei," "Du, du liegst mir im Herzen" ("You, You Are in My Heart"), and "Ach wie ist's möglich dann" ("Oh, How Is It Possible Then").

Our desks and seats in school were the old-fashioned, two-passenger variety. Boys and girls always paired off separately. The front part of the unit was the seat, and the back part was the desk top for the seat behind. Under the desk tops were compartments for books and school supplies. One drawback to the double desks was that there never was enough space for two kids, but a worse problem was the strange coincidence that the pupils in front invariably wiggled just when we were doing our penmanship or art, and as a result our penmanship took on a scribbled effect and our art, a doodled look. The larger desks for the older pupils were in the back, and from there the desks got smaller toward the front in stair-step fashion. The longer you stayed in school, the farther back you were promoted. It was a sort of progression in reverse. Between the teacher's desk in front of the room and the pupils' seats was the recitation bench. The different classes were called up by grade and subject, and they came forward to demonstrate their knowledge while the others remained at their desks or did work at the blackboard.

My first teacher was a robust young man with a broad smile that reached from ear to ear and with a bass voice that boomed like a big tuba in a brass band. His name was Sam Hoerster. I thought he was at least as strong as, if not stronger than, Samson. He had attended Blinn College, a small German Methodist school in Brenham, Texas. On the first day of school I was as scared as a little boy suddenly confronted by a big brown bear. Sam Hoerster eased our fears by saying "Guten Morgen" and calling us by our first names. When I started to school in 1910, there were fifty-three pupils enrolled, ten of these in my beginners' class. We were all grandchildren of German pioneer families. At one time there were several Mexican families in our neighborhood whose children attended our school, too, but there were no Anglo-American families represented during my time.

The majority of my teachers in the little rural school were men. It is difficult for me to think of these men teachers as elementary instructors, but they drilled the ABC's, the multiplication tables, and children's verses like "Twinkle, Twinkle, Little Star" and "Mary Had a Little Lamb" into our heads.

Otto Moerner was my second teacher, and I kept a copy of a souvenir folder of 1912 that he gave to all his pupils at the end of school. On the front of the folder is his picture, showing a neat, well-dressed young man. On the inside are printed the names of his forty-four pupils in the Plehweville Public School, District No. 6. The printer managed to misspell Plehweville, and it came out as Plehwville. On the list of names I find two Dannheims, three Donops, three Eckerts, three Hasses, six Hoersters, ten Jordans, eight Leifestes, one Moerner, two Pluennekes, two Standkes, two Vaters, and two Willmanns. After a few years the trustees brought back an experienced schoolmaster, Christian Leifeste. He had taught this same school earlier for a period of thirteen years. He was a descendant of one of the early German-Methodist settlers, and he was one of the few rural-school teachers of his day who devoted an entire lifetime to his profession.

Most of our instructors received meager salaries and stayed only about a year before they moved on to greener pastures. Originally the teachers were paid by state funds for only part of the year. This aid sufficed for about five months. The rest of the year it was a private school, and the teachers had to assess the parents the necessary amounts per month per pupil and then collect the money themselves. A few pupils always dropped out of school when tuition had to be paid.

Only two of my teachers stayed as long as two years. Besides Christian Leifeste, the other one was Milda Eckert, my fifth teacher. She was fresh out of Southwest Texas Normal Institute at San Marcos. In later years she prided herself on having given me a good foundation in German. My next teacher was sweet little Kate Gay. She was a graduate of that small, half-defunct Methodist school named Cherokee Junior College, at Cherokee, Texas. She had also attended Southern Methodist University at Dallas. She was our second Anglo teacher. Though she knew a little classroom German, she did not teach us any because she pronounced the little German she knew with an American accent.

During her tenure as teacher, we had a country-school box supper. The girls prepared pretty boxes with all kinds of good food inside, wrapped the boxes in colorful crepe paper, and tied gay ribbons around them. Then on some festive evening, after the county judge, who was ex-officio county school superintendent, had made a speech, the boxes were auctioned off to the highest bidders among the boys. Some of them managed to buy their girl friends' boxes, but others got stung. Interestingly, though, some of those boys who did get stung found their future mates through miscalculation or accident and later lived happily ever after with their box-supper partners. After the boxes were auctioned off, most of the couples sat down together and ate their suppers in the schoolroom, but some of them went outside to the steps or to the water well and ate in the dark and perhaps sandwiched in a little courting.

The box supper brought in so much money that after Miss Kate purchased some needed school equipment, she had money left to buy little personal gifts for all the pupils. The girls promptly chose ribbons, cheap rings or bracelets, or perhaps folding Japanese fans. But what can boys choose as gifts? Finally one of us had a brilliant idea. We would request water pistols. With innocent faces we proposed our seemingly innocuous choice. Miss Kate thought it was a clever idea. What could nice, clean water hurt on a warm day, even if it was shot from a pistol?

All went well at first, but when we began to mix red ink with our water ammunition, Miss Kate took every water pistol and all the red ink into custody. That ended the squirting, and we turned out to be model pupils for fear that our teacher would tell our parents. And they would have reddened our buttocks without the aid of red ink.

Eli Dechert, my last teacher in the country school, once did me a great favor. He took me along on a trip to Fredericksburg, the western capital of the German Texas Hill Country. This was a sort of field trip long before the days of such excursions. He had an early-vintage Model T Ford, the kind that had magneto ignition. I'll never forget the rhythmic clicking of the four coils there with us in the front passenger compartment. The roads were sandy in places and rough in others. Eli often had to press the left or low-gear pedal that was vibrating along with the whole triumvirate of floor pedals. The motor growled and the water in the brass-covered radiator boiled, but we made it past the *Hausberg* (the "House Mountain"), up the steep grade of the *Lochberg* (literally, the "mountain with the hole"), and past the *Kreuzberg* (the "Cross Mountain"). I did not know before then how "bergy" that part of the country really is. Finally we chugged into town along Main Street, drove past the courthouse and the spot where the rebuilt *Kaffeemühle* ("coffee mill") building now stands, and came to Eli's parental home.

I did not know these people very well, even though they were my relatives, because they lived in a foreign world that was unfamiliar to me. Although my grandfather was one of the first settlers in Fredericksburg in 1846 and lived there for ten years, the town was virtually unknown to me. The Fredericksburg German element was and still is more fun-loving, more easy-going than the Mason County Methodists. The Fredericksburgers love their *Gemütlichkeit*, their easy-going disposition and geniality, as much as the Mason County Methodists love their piety.

Bilingual education was characteristic of most German towns and communities in Texas during the nineteenth and early part of the twentieth centuries. The Institute of Texan Cultures in San Antonio emphasizes this fact by proclaiming on a large poster, "Every German community had at least an elementary school and pioneered a bilingual, bicultural education." This "German-English education was based on a sound curriculum in mathematics, history, literature, languages, and music, conducted in German and English."

In our little bilingual school we got a good exposure to both English and German, at least until 1918, when German instruction in public schools ended because of World War I. Although the community was predominantly a German settlement, the school curriculum was primarily Anglo-American. To be sure, the people wanted to keep their German heritage and language, but they also realized that for their own good and for the good of their new fatherland they must become well integrated into American life.

Around the turn of the century, it was still easy to keep the knowledge of German alive. It was spoken at home and was the children's first language. Moreover, most of the teachers were bilingual; thus it was quite simple for them, while stressing English first, to teach the children to read German in the Gothic letters and to write the difficult, old-fashioned German script or *Handschrift*, something that has become so archaic that it is practically a lost art.

Here is a sample of the German script we learned in school:

This reads in print:

> Der Mai ist gekommen,
> Die Bäume schlagen aus,
> Da bleibe, wer Lust hat,
> Mit Sorgen zu Haus!

> (May has come,
> The trees are budding out;
> Let him who wishes
> Stay at home with his gout [literally, cares]!)

Not very much time was actually given to German instruction, but we got a good background in linguistic, literary, and folkloric material. Some of our teachers had us memorize little poems and ditties that I never forgot. Much of this material was found in our textbooks and readers; for example:

> A, B, C [pronounced *Ah, Bay, Tsay*],
> Die Katze lief im Schnee [pronounced *Schnay*].
> Und als sie wieder 'raus kam,
> Da hatt' sie weisse Zeh' [pronounced *Tsay*].

With some alphabetical license, I can translate this verse as follows:

> M, N, O,
> The cat ran in the snow;
> And when she came out again,
> She had a white toe.

Here is another little gem we learned in school:

> "Muh, muh," ruft die Kuh.
> Wir geben ihr das Futter;
> Sie gibt uns Milch und Butter.
> "Muh, muh," ruft die Kuh.

I have racked my brain mercilessly, but I simply cannot come up with any acceptable rhymes; so we will do without them:

> "Moo, moo," calls the cow.
> We give her feed and fodder;
> She gives us milk and butter.
> "Moo, moo," calls the cow.

If a cow were still called a *cu*, as in thirteenth-century English, then the word would rhyme with *moo*. And if those old Anglo-Saxons who invented the English language had called *fodder* simply *futter*, we would have a rhyming word to go with *butter*. As it is, we got cheated out of several good rhyming words. On the other hand, we would have lost other rhymes, and nobody could have coined the phrase "How, now, brown cow."

Quoting animal language reminds me that a donkey brays *Hee-haw* in English but *I-a* (pronounced *Ee-ah*) in German, and an American rooster crows *Cock-a-doodle-doo*, while his German cousin proclaims *Ki-ke-ri-ki*. This comes as no surprise when you stop to think that we human beings give the animals a bad example with our amazing diversity of language.

We also read some of the shorter *Märchen* ("fairy tales") by the Brothers Grimm, among them, "Die Wichtelmänner" ("The Elves"), and "Hans im Glücke" ("Hans in Luck"), and some fables by Aesop, Lessing, and Gleim. All these stories and poems were in our German textbooks. We began with a little German primer (*Fibel*), and then we used a series of eclectic readers and grammars by Weick and Greber, called *Deutsches Erstes Lesebuch, Zweites Lesebuch*, and *Drittes Lesebuch* ("German First Reader," "Second Reader," and "Third Reader"). These books were published by the American Book Company of Cincinnati, which also published another book we used, H. H. Fick's *Hin und Her: Ein Buch für Kinder* ("From Here and There: A Book for Children").

In our English classes we read everything we found in our text-books, which were late adaptations of the old *McGruder Eclectic Readers*. Longfellow was always well represented, and we not only read, but also memorized, many of his poems, such as his "Village Blacksmith," "Sail on, O Ship of State," and "The Psalm of Life." When we were little, we enjoyed Whittier's "The Barefoot Boy" be-cause we could identify with the "little man," in spite of the poet's use of the Quaker *thou*, *thy*, and *thee*:

> Blessings on thee, little man,
> Barefoot boy, with cheeks of tan!
> With thy turned-up pantaloons,
> And thy merry whistled tunes;
> With thy red lips, redder still
> Kissed by strawberries on the hill.

There were various stories in our readers, but I have forgotten most of them. I do remember the fairy tale, "The King of the Golden River." Mr. Ruskin, the author, should feel posthumously flattered for that. And there was some tale about lapwings, but who ever heard of lapwings in central Texas? Chaparral birds or roadrunners, *Ja*, but lapwings, *Nein*! We also had simplified versions of some of the Greek stories by Homer, but all this was far removed in time and place from Plehweville, Texas, which was still a semifrontier cow country. We also read some of the Grimm Brothers' German fairy tales in English, no doubt with some of the grimness deleted.

Everybody got his dose of grammar in the language courses. It was fun to learn the principal parts of irregular verbs with their re-lated nouns: "sing, sang, sung, the song; stink, stank, stunk, the stench; see, saw, seen, the sight; do, did, done, the deed." For German-English speakers this sing-song melody is doubly pleasant because of the similarity between German and English. Compare the English forms of the above with the German verbs: *singen, sang, gesungen, der Gesang; stinken, stank, gestunken, der Gestank; sehen, sah, gesehen, die (Aus)sicht; tun, tat, getan, die Tat*. These sounds are all pleasant and easy to remember.

We had a series of beautiful art-literature readers, and they gave me my first glimpse into the field of great paintings. These were extraordinary books with prints from paintings by French, German,

English, Dutch, and Italian artists. I can still see Rosa Bonheur's "Horse Fair" picture, among others.

There were the usual geography books: *Texas Geography* in the fifth grade, *World Geography* in the seventh, and *Physical Geography* in the eighth. The books were not too imaginative, but we got something of a school-book perspective of the world through maps, many good illustrations, and pictures. We memorized the names of states and capitals, of rivers and mountain ranges, of oceans and seas, but we really did not get a very good concept of our immediate surroundings, and the outside world was too far away. Fortunately, though, we were well oriented because our seats faced north, and we saw our maps with the north side up.

Texas history came in the sixth grade. We used the Barker, Potts, and Ramsdell textbook, *A School History of Texas.* We liked Texas history because it came close to home, but the textbook had little or nothing to say about the German immigration that had populated large areas of Texas from Galveston and Houston in the east, through Brenham, LaGrange, Giddings, Schulenburg, Yorktown, Seguin, New Braunfels, San Antonio, Castroville, Boerne, Comfort, and Fredericksburg, and on to Mason. Although we lived at one end of this German Belt and were part of it, our teachers never mentioned it in school. United States history came in the seventh grade. It was one of my favorite subjects, and I never lost my interest in history.

In our mathematics courses there was definitely no "new math." We memorized our multiplication tables, recited them, and wrote them many times. We added and subtracted our way through a whole series of dull books in the usual old-fashioned way. Since we had to apply our memory work to stated problems, we particularly enjoyed the riddle-problem that states: "If there are five birds sitting on a fence and a boy shoots one, how many are left?" The answer is, of course, "None. The others would fly away." The German version of this arithmetic riddle, which is found in our *Hin und Her* book, reads:

> Es sassen zehn Sperlinge auf dem Dach;
> Da kam ein Jäger und schoss danach;
> Er traf davon nur vier.
> Wie viele blieben sitzen?
> Das sage mir!

(Ten sparrows were sitting on the roof;
A hunter came and shot: "Poof, poof!"
He hit of them but four.
How many were sitting then?
Tell me that and more.)

Such riddles were a part of our school life, and we were intrigued by them. We even got a double dose of riddles, in English and in German. Sometimes both versions were rhymed, as is the custom in children's verses. Here is an English version of a familiar riddle:

> First white as snow,
> Then green as clover,
> Then red as blood,
> Tastes good all over.

The German version, with the full *a,a,b,b* rhyme scheme, looks like the original:

> Erst weiss wie Schnee,
> Dann grün wie Klee,
> Dann rot wie Blut,
> Schmeckt allen Kindern gut.

The answer is *Eine Kirsche* ("a cherry"), but we always gave *Eine Pflaume* ("a plum") as the answer, because we had no cherries in Texas.

We also knew a number of counting-out verses (*Abzählverse*) or games, in English and in German, but the little rhymed lines are sometimes quite different in the two languages. Nevertheless, they were used for the same purpose. A close parallel to the English "Eeney, meeney, miney, mo" is:

> Ene, dene, Tintenfass ("ink well"),
> Geh zur Schul' und lerne was.
> Wenn du was gelernet hast,
> Komm nach Haus und sag' mir das.
> Eins, zwei, drei: du bist frei.

> (Eeny, meeney, school bells ring,
> Go to school and learn a thing.
> When you've learned a thing or two,
> Come and tell me, right and true.
> One, two, three: you are free.)

A better known counting-out poem is "Ich und du und Müllers Kuh; / Bäckers Esel, das bist du" ("I and thou, and Miller's cow; / Baker's donkey, that art thou").

Of course, we learned the familiar English rhyme that goes as follows:

> One, two, three, four, five;
> I caught a hare alive.
> Six, seven, eight, nine, ten;
> I let him go again.

There are many German verses like this that count to three, five, and seven. Here is one that everybody knew:

> Eins, zwei, drei, vier, fünf, sechs, sieben;
> Wo ist denn mein Schatz geblieben?
> Ist nicht hier, ist nicht da;
> Ist wohl in Amerika.

> (One, two, three, four, five, six, seven;
> Has my sweetheart gone to heaven?
> Is not here, is not there;
> Must be in America, fair.)

Both German and English have their tongue-twisters like "Peter Piper picked a peck of pickled peppers." Our favorite in German is just about as hard in English: "Fischers Fritz fischt frische Fische; / Frische Fische fischt Fischers Fritz" ("Fisher's Fritz fishes fresh fish; / Fresh fish fishes Fischer's Fritz").

The best nonsensical German ditty I can remember goes as follows:

> Fritz, Stiegelitz,
> Dein Vogel ist tot;
> Liegt unter dem Baum
> Und frisst kein Brot.

> (Fritz, Stiegelitz,
> Your birdie is dead;
> Lies under the tree
> And eats no bread.)

The teachers of the early one-room, rural schools relaxed on Friday afternoons and put on spelling matches. Sides were chosen, the pupils lined up on opposite walls, and the battle started. Some of the kids whose orthography was permanently shaky always went down immediately when it came to words like *raccoon, rattlesnake, mesquite, Methodist,* or *Plehweville.* On the other hand, some kids, eager beavers, could spell all the words in the Webster's blue-back spellers.

I still like that "Blue Back" name, but Noah Webster, the author, called the book *American Spelling-Book,* and one of the revisions was called *The Elementary Spelling-Book.* It too had the familiar blue back, but there is nothing elementary about it. Besides endless rules on spelling, pronunciation, and syllabification, the book contains some of the most monstrous words in Webster's unabridged dictionary. They are all listed with the proper division into syllables in this blue-back speller. I was really quite wrong when I asserted above that some of the eager beavers could spell all the words in the blue-back spellers. Nobody could do that but Noah Webster. When the teachers got tired of the spelling match, they simply called out words like *pu-sil-lan-i-mous,* and the whole affair was ended; it was sudden death to the spelling match. Thank goodness, we never had to define these words. As sure as not, the teachers themselves did not know the meanings of some of them. Even Doctor Webster reserved the definitions for his dictionary.

Recently some friends showed me their mother's well-worn blue-back speller, and I saw what Noah Webster provided in place of definitions. He composed hundreds of isolated sentences, illustrating the use of the words. He did not mean to be funny, but the odd collection of sentences will call forth smiles among present-day readers. Here are a few of these gems: "a cross cat will scratch with her sharp nails," "the little sister can knit a pair of garters," and "a loquacious companion is sometimes a great torment."

I found one great desecration in the little blue-back book, not by Doctor Webster, heaven forbid! Some early user of the book, who got into the spirit of the sentences perfectly but failed to heed Webster's rules on spelling, added his own version and orthography when he wrote in pencil on page 115, "Mary is a scunk."

In my days in school, we did not use the genuine blue-back spellers anymore. Our spelling books still had blue backs all right, but they had been pedagogically streamlined, with the words graded and put in smaller learning units. And best of all, the unmanageable words had been eliminated.

My brothers and sisters and I walked the two short miles to school when the weather was not too bad or the Willow Creek was not flowing too broad a stream. Our usual fellow pedestrians were our neighbors' children, the Standkes: Paul, Minna, Bertha, and Gus. We had an interesting shortcut trail that led across the pastures, the Willow Creek, and the pecan bottoms. The creek crossing was always fun, whether the sand was dry and crunchy or wet, boggy, and partly covered by a stream of clear water. In winter we usually walked across on a low, log bridge. In warm weather we waded barefoot through the cool water.

In the pastures we walked through the soft grasses and past the colorful flowers—bluebonnets, wild phlox, wine cups (we called them *Glockenblumen*, "bell flowers"), and daisies—provided the sheep had not already eaten all of them. We saw birds like field larks, sparrows, woodpeckers, mockingbirds, doves, buzzards, roadrunners, hawks, and cardinals. Occasionally, we encountered wild animals, little harmless ones like lizards, prairie snakes, rabbits and squirrels, and sometimes a rare deer or two, as well as grazing cattle and sheep and rooting hogs.

When we were little, we were always half-afraid that we might meet a wolf or a coyote, but they never showed us either their faces or their teeth. Most of the children had been warned and frightened of wolves by their mothers. This may have been part of the parents' European background and the "Little Red Riding Hood" tradition, which had a telling effect on children's imagination. On one occasion, one of the little boys, Warren Dannheim was his name, reported excitedly when he arrived at school, "I almost saw a wolf this morning."

It was fun to walk through the pecan grove, especially in the autumn when the pecans were falling. We bent down many times and filled our pockets or lunch pails with pecans. We had no German word for *pecan*, nor did our dictionaries, so when we talked German among ourselves, we simply called them *Nüsse* ("nuts"). Another pleasure in autumn, when the brown and yellow leaves were falling, was kicking aside the pecan foliage from our footpath or just running along and wading through deep drifts of light-weight leaves.

The children who lived at greater distances from school drove in one-horse buggies. We never used the verb *to ride* when we spoke of buggies, wagons, and hacks. We restricted this verb to riding horses, wild steers, and donkeys. We always *drove* in our buggies, and this was part of our bilingual heritage. The German verb *reiten* always means to ride an animal, but the verb *fahren* (compare English "fare") means to ride or drive a vehicle, and this determined our usage.

There are many interesting tales and strange happenings associated with the horse-and-buggy era. If a boy wanted to get into favor with a pretty country girl, he hitched and unhitched her horse at school and fed the horse its corn-top fodder. It was not that the girls were unable to do these things, for they always did them at home; it was simply one of the few gallantries that the boys could perform. We called our girl friends *Schatz* ("sweetheart," really "treasure") in German, and our Anglo friends thought we said "shots." By the time I came along, the old tricks of fodder and hitching did not work too well any more. The best we could do was to stand around like wooden Indians until somebody broke the ice and said, "Du bist mein Schatz" ("You are my sweetheart"). When we were too bashful to make such a bold declaration and could only put on a silly grin, we wrote notes in school and passed them along in books, notes like "I love you, Lillie," or "Milton loves Minnie," or "Ben loves Bertha."

My brothers and sisters and I drove to school in bad weather only, provided old Blue, our balking horse, cooperated. Sometimes when he was cold-shouldered, he went in reverse when we wanted to go forward. That was always a frightening experience. Later we discovered that deep down in his dear old equestrian heart Blue was not really a balker but a "goer." He merely insisted on being the first to go. Whenever he couldn't be first, he began to sulk, throw a temper tantrum, and go into reverse. The solution to the problem was to hitch up Blue during the afternoon recess. Then as soon as school was out, we untied the would-be race horse, jumped into the buggy as quickly as possible, and Blue started off like a scared jackrabbit while the other horses were still being hitched up. Blue was a "goer" all right, and when you let him go, he took you home in a blue streak.

While talking about horses and buggies and fodder, we should also mention "horse apples." I don't mean the green, nubby apples which grow on bois d'arc trees. No, I mean horse droppings, produced by horses that eat dry, corn-top fodder all day long at school. We called these droppings *Pferdeknittel* in German, but a more imaginative word would be *Pferdeäpfel*, which translates into "horse apples." These processed hay "apples" tend to harden in a few days in a dry climate, and they make an excellent substitute for snowballs.

We selected the driest specimens of horse apples and had a pitched battle during one noon recess. One group of boys defended the "fort," the schoolhouse, while the other group, the "Indians," made the attack and fired from positions behind trees and buggies. No one was hurt, but our battlefield, including the schoolhouse, became a disaster area.

When "Professor" Christian Leifeste returned from lunch, which he ate regularly with his family in his nearby home, which we called the "teacherage," he seized us warriors, Indians and Rangers alike, and marched us into prison while the innocent little girls, whose horses had furnished us with our ammunition, watched the maneuver and giggled. Then Professor Leifeste corralled us boys, provided us with brooms and, in the presence of the giggling girls, made us give the schoolroom the most thorough cleanup it had received in over a year. If there ever was a case of fitting the punishment to the crime, this was it. The episode made a lasting impression on us, and it was definitely a portion of our education. One thing is sure, Christian Leifeste made Christians out of a bunch of "wild Indians" much faster than some of the preachers at the camp meetings could have done.

We carried our books and school supplies in large, homemade satchels made of heavy, dark-gray, striped cotton material. They had flaps that could be buttoned down and shoulder straps for carrying. In my family we carried lunch in old-fashioned metal dinner pails, while others used Arbuckle-coffee or Union-Leader-tobacco cans. Our mothers prepared sandwiches of homemade bread, butter, and jam, and we carried chunks of *Kochkäse*, *Handkäse*, smoked *Wurst*, fruits in season, hard-boiled eggs, tomatoes, and cookies. When we did not eat all of our sandwiches (German *Butterbrote*) but brought some back home, Mother called them *Hasenbrote* ("rabbit bread" or sandwiches), and we had to eat them later. She did not let us waste food at any time.

For school lunches when the weather was good, as it usually was, we sat down on the ground or on rocks in the shade of trees or by the water well and gulped down our food as fast as possible so that we would have time to play. In cold weather we sought out the sunny side of the school building, or we built a large fire on the school grounds to keep us warm.

Most of the school children carried folding or collapsible drinking cups in their dinner pails or in their pockets. We drew drinking water by the bucketful from the old well by the schoolhouse. This well had a brown sandstone curbing and a large, solid stone slab on top with a three-foot hole chiseled through it. Overhead was a U-shaped frame with a pulley for the rope and buckets. After we learned about germs in our yellow book on health and hygiene, we no longer drank directly from the bucket or from the cups fastened to the well by little chains. Most of the ranchmen did not believe in germs, because no one had ever seen any of them on the ranches, but our mothers made us carry our own aluminum folding cups anyway.

We also carried pocket knives and used them to shell the pecans during fall and winter. We did not crack the pecans; we carved a complete longitudinal belt line around the nuts. Then we lifted out the perfect halves of the kernels. Whenever we were not mad at the girls for excelling us in schoolwork, we shared a few nut meats with them. During the fall and winter the thumbs of all boys bore marks and scars from the constant contact with the sharp edge of the knife blade and the chopped pecan shells. Our pocket knives were a real necessity in school. We had no pencil sharpeners, so we whittled away the wood from the lead of the pencils. This was so much fun that we whittled away more than was necessary, and our parents must have thought we ate pencils. The boys could always impress the girls by sharpening their pencils or shelling pecans for them, and the girls could show which boys they loved by asking them to perform these services.

We had midmorning, noon, and midafternoon recesses, during which we went out on the playground and played various games. At school-starting time every morning and at the end of each recess, the teacher rang a hand bell to call the children into the schoolroom. The sound of the brass bell was clear and pleasant, not raucous like that of modern electric bells.

The girls had a four-passenger privy or *Häuschen* ("little house"), as we called this rural outhouse with its Sears-Roebuck catalogue, where they could go during recess. The boys went down the banks of the Willow Creek or behind trees and bushes. This was the typical arrangement for Texas rural schools and churches. We were fortunate to have the banks of the creek and groves of trees to hide us. I wonder what the boys did in the schools on the treeless plains.

We played games in the morning and afternoon recesses and during the noon hour. We called one of these games *Mummela*, but in other parts of the German Belt it was called *Sautreiben* ("sow driving"). Before playing this game, we dug a number of six-inch holes or pits in the ground in a circle, one hole for each participant, less one, and one larger hole in the center. All the players had three-foot sticks or pegs, and they stuck them into the center hole and marched around, mumbling, "Mummela, mummela, mummela." Outside the circle was a crushed tin-can ball. At some moment in the circular marching and chanting a signal was given, and all the boys made a dash for the outside holes and stuck their sticks into the holes. The odd player, who failed to make good his claim to one of the holes, was "it." His task was to knock the angular ball or "sow" into one of the holes on the outside or into the center hole. Everybody defended the territory with his stick or maul, provided he did not get mauled first. If the can landed in one of the holes or if the attacker stuck his stick into it while the defender tried to beat the can away, the loser was "it," and so it went on. I don't remember what the rewards or the spoils of the battle were, probably none, but the penalty was that you got your shins smashed.

We also played baseball. The big boys used regulation horsehide balls, gloves, mitts, masks, belly protectors, and bats, and they played a hard game. The older boys handed down used balls to the little boys, but these secondhand balls still had enough life in them to knock out small boys. None of us wanted to be the catcher, and those who were conscripted to play this position usually stood way back where they might stop the pitched ball on first or second hop. When we inherited a catcher's mitt from the big boys, we decided that our catchers should take their position right behind the batters, just as the big boys did. But we had no catcher's mask, so the first deflected speed ball hit our catcher on his forehead, and he was too dazed to continue. After this blow, he again stood way back, well out of reach of a swinging bat or a deflected ball.

We also indulged in a number of simple games and contests, such as footracing, jumping, wrestling, rock throwing, horseshoe and washer pitching, and mumblety peg. In the early days the boys and girls were not allowed to play together, but by the time I came along, the girls joined in with the boys in such games as anty-over, stink base, crack the whip, townball, blackman, and red rover. In playing crack the whip, the bigger boys and girls always asserted a sort of priority by claiming the head of the line, while the small fry got the tail end, where they were flung around until they landed dizzily in the dirt and bawled.

The boys enjoyed playing leapfrog, the familiar game in which you take turns jumping, with legs spread wide, over the bent backs of others. One trouble with this game was that some of the bigger boys were so accustomed to jumping on horses and riding them bareback that they sometimes jumped on the squatting fellow in front and rode him like a horse until he sank down to the ground, exhausted. This usually broke up the game and occasionally resulted in a fight. The bigger girls might have joined in this game with the boys, but they wore such long skirts that they could not have jumped over anything or anybody.

The game that had a lot of local color for the Willow Creek community might be called "swinging in the willows." It was easy to learn; all we had to do was to climb up into the branches of a willow tree and then start swaying back and forth, until we took the stiffness out of them, as Robert Frost said about birches. We could all climb well, that was no problem, but the swinging was something like riding a pitching bronco. All went well as long as each boy had a tree or limb to himself, but all too often the bigger boys wanted to climb onto an already occupied limb and shake the smaller kids out, about the same way we knew how to shake an opossum out of a tree. There were plenty of "dropouts" in the game, but fortunately we usually landed on all fours, like a cat. The sand and the Bermuda grass were soft, so our landings were not much of a jolt. Swinging in the willows was really a great game; to paraphrase Frost, one could do worse than be a swinger of willows.

The school year always came to a close with a parade from the school to the pecan bottoms, about a mile down the Willow Creek, where we had our school picnics every spring. We decorated a wagon and perhaps a few hacks and buggies with bright-colored crepe paper. Some of the boys and a few girls on sidesaddles rode their horses decked out with ribbons and paper flowers on saddles and bridles. Then we moved in a gay procession, led by mounted flag bearers, to the picnic grounds, singing, shouting, and talking.

Our parents and our older and younger brothers and sisters, uncles and aunts, and friends awaited our arrival at the picnic grounds. Here the school patrons had built a wooden platform for our program and wooden benches for the spectators. We school children presented a program of songs that we had learned in school. The small children usually recited German poems like "Klaus ist in den Wald gegangen, weil er will die Vöglein fangen" ("Klaus has gone into the woods because he wants to catch the birds") and "Fuchs, du hast die Gans gestohlen" ("Fox, you have stolen the goose"). There were also recitations of English poems, such as Longfellow's "Under the spreading chestnut tree the village smithy stands." Some pupil usually orated the "Concord Hymn" and tried to impress the Texas ranchmen with this poem about the "embattled farmers" of 1775.

We also gave simple skits or pantomime acts. I remember the time when my classmates and I got dressed in mouse costumes with big ears and long tails and acted out the "Three Blind Mice" song. I cannot remember just how the farmer's wife manipulated the butcher knife and the tail-cutting act, but we escaped without injury. My sister Emily once acted in a pantomime of "Backward, Turn Backward, O Time in Thy Flight." Since she was still a very little girl with not too much time behind her, she was lucky that time did not turn backward too far. She might have been backed completely out of existence.

Some of our teachers put us through a schoolroom recitation routine on the stage. This was one way we could share our knowledge with our parents and the teachers could impress the school patrons. In election years, there would also be several candidates who were all too eager to address the people and break down the voter's apathy.

About fifty yards from the platform was a refreshment stand where we could buy soda pop in various colors and flavors. The stand also had a big crock full of refreshing, yellow lemonade. In addition to soda pop and lemonade, the stand keeper sold chewing gum, popcorn, homemade ice cream, and candy for the children. We had no German word for *candy*, so we said *Kändie*. For the men and older boys there were cigars and chewing tobacco. To this day, the smell of cigar smoke out in the open air reminds me of school picnics in the pecan bottoms, and to this day I think smoking and chewing tobacco are outdoor sports. At noon our lunch was served on the ground.

In the afternoon we had footraces, tree-climbing contests, wading in the Willow Creek, and hiking in the woods. The men either sat around and smoked cigars and chewed tobacco, or they pitched horseshoes and dollars. There was not too much folding money floating about, but all the men carried silver dollars in money purses. The main event of the afternoon was a baseball game in my father's pasture, where the big boys had cleared away some bushes, mesquite trees, and cactus and had marked off a baseball diamond in the grass. When the game ended, the picnic was over and we left. Going home at the end of the day had a touch of sadness about it. We were leaving our playmates and going home for a summer of hard work on the farm or ranch.

My little brown schoolhouse still stands, but it is much changed. The warm-colored stone with the broad, white chalk mortar trowelled in between the stones looked cheerful and inviting, especially when the mortar had been freshly refurbished. But replacing the mortar was a technical craft, and not too many ranchmen were skilled in this work. No one but Henry or Theodor Brockmann or Ernest Vater would undertake this job, so it was inevitable that after their deaths nobody refinished and refreshed the white mortar. Instead the pretty walls were plastered over with ugly gray cement in a stucco effect. With this treatment the building lost all its personality. Then, after the schools in Mason County were consolidated, the children rode to the central schools in the town of Mason in yellow school buses with vile fuel odors. Gone are the good old horse-and-buggy days and the fodder and horse-apple fragrance. The little building is now spending its old age and retirement as a community center, and it has an appropriate state historical building marker proclaiming its former glory.

7

From Christmas to Water Witching

MANY traditions were brought to the Texas Hill Country by the German colonists, and some of these practices have lived on to the present day. The most striking of these are the Christmas and Easter customs, but much additional *Kulturerbe* ("cultural heritage") was perpetuated by the German settlers in Texas, such as the practices pertaining to holidays, greeting cards and *Stammbücher* ("memory albums"), weddings, proverbs, godparents, handshaking, children's songs and poems, family reunions and genealogical studies, home remedies, folk beliefs, weather signs, water witching, faith healing, pranks, and spooks.

Many of our American Christmas customs can be traced back to Europe, especially to Germany and Holland. For example, Santa Claus comes from *Sankt Nikolaus*, Kriss Kringle derives from *Christkindlein*, "the little Christ child," although the name is applied to a different character in America than it was in the Old World, and the Christmas tree (German *Tannenbaum*, "fir tree") was brought to America by German and Dutch settlers. Several favorite Christmas songs brought over by the Germans have lived on in the Texas Hill Country and elsewhere in German neighborhoods.

The religious element comes to light primarily in two church activities that were particularly characteristic of German communities: the church service (*Gottesdienst*) on Christmas day and the evening Christmas program, given primarily by and for the children and the young people. In the worship service, one of our favorite songs was "O du selige, o du fröhliche," the first stanza of which reads:

> O du selige, o du fröhliche,
> Gnadenbringende Weihnachtszeit!
> Welt ging verloren,

> Christ ward geboren:
> Freue, freue dich, o Christenheit!
> *(Gesangbuch, 59)*

My unrhymed translation can be sung to the original Sicilian melody:

> O thou blesséd, o thou joyful,
> Mercy-bringing Christmastide!
> Lost were all people,
> Christ came to save us:
> Oh, rejoice ye, all Christendom.

We also sang "Silent Night, Holy Night" in the original German, as it was written and composed by Joseph Mohr and Franz Gruber. Later I learned the English translation, but to this day I still prefer the original German. Here is the first stanza:

> Stille Nacht, heilige Nacht!
> Alles schläft, einsam wacht
> Nur das traute, hochheilige Paar.
> Holder Knabe im lockigen Haar,
> Schlaf' in himmlischer Ruh',
> Schlaf' in himmlischer Ruh'.
> (Bacon, p. 129)

Then the preacher delivered his annual Christmas sermon.

The children's Christmas program was characteristic of the German settlements. It began with the singing of German Christmas carols by all. After the songs and the scripture reading, the pastor and the Sunday-school superintendent spoke a few words. Then came the children's program, which usually interested the people most of all. A month or so before Christmas, the Sunday-school superintendent appointed a committee to arrange the children's evening. All children received poems and other material to memorize, and they recited these religious verses and sang little songs with a Biblical and a Christ-Child theme. One of the better known poems and songs of this kind, the "Christkindlein" ("The Little Christ Child"), begins with the following verses:

> Alle Jahre wieder
> Kommt das Christuskind
> Auf die Erde nieder,
> Wo wir Menschen sind.

(Every year again
Comes the Christ Child
Down to earth below
Where we humans are.)

Along with the religious poems and songs, nonreligious elements also entered in. One Santa Claus song, sung to the tune of "Twinkle, Twinkle, Little Star," begins as follows in German:

Morgen kommt der Weihnachtsmann,
Kommt mit seinen Gaben.

(Tomorrow comes old Santa Claus,
Comes with all his presents.)

I still remember a little *Weihnachtsmann* ("Santa Claus") poem I recited:

Der Weihnachtsmann ist ein guter Mann;
Er bringt den Kleinen, was er kann.
Die Grossen lässt er laufen;
Die könn'n sich selbst was kaufen.

(Santa Claus is a good old man;
He brings the children all he can.
The grown-ups he will leave alone;
They buy their presents on their own.)

The highlights of the evening were the large Christmas tree and the receiving of paper bags filled with fruits and sweets. In our community the tree always was a freshly cut cedar or juniper tree, so large that ladders were used in decorating it. In the earlier days, before the turn of the century, the tree was decorated with apples, wax candles, and homemade cookies.

After edible decorations were no longer hung on the tree, these goodies were handed out individually in large paper bags. A committee of young people collected money, bought oranges, apples, candy, and paper bags (*Tüten*). Then they wrote the names of all the church members and their children on individual bags and put ample portions of the *Bescherung* ("gifts") into all the bags. To provide refreshments for visitors and nonmembers, a number of unlabeled bags were also prepared. The filled bags were placed under the decorated tree. After the children's program was over, the people remained seated while the committee members distributed the bags. After they got their goodies, most people ate some of their refreshments in the church before going home.

One of the most enjoyable pre-Christmas activities was at home: the baking and decorating of Christmas cookies. My mother and sisters baked the cookies in the shape of stars, doughnuts, birds, ducks, horses, Santa Clauses, Christmas trees, and toys. Then the entire family gathered around the dining table and decorated the cookies. They were first covered with a layer of white icing, then with colored icing we drew all kinds of designs on them—eyes, wings, neck bands, faces, legs, tree limbs, and various abstract shapes—or we strewed colored sugar and other decorations on the fresh icings.

Sometime between December 6 and Christmas Eve, *Sankt Niko-laus* came to check up on the little children. We were afraid of this stern European character, but we usually escaped his wrath and switch when our parents vouched for our goodness and we said our prayers before him. Then he gave us some treats and called us good children. Sister Hulda tells of a visit by this unsaintly saint with his threatening switch. She and her sisters were half-grown teenagers, well beyond the days of childish pranks, when this character appeared. The girls recognized the fellow and refused to kneel and say their prayers. When the stupid St. Nicholas started to punish the girls, they ran off and hid in the cellar, where he couldn't find them. Of course, they could have unmasked the inept Nicholas, but they did not want us little kids to see his true face and lose our faith, especially after we had already said our prayers.

Another pre-Christmas activity was hunting and cutting the cedar trees. We had a ranch in the Blue Mountains, about twenty-five miles from home, where cedar or juniper trees grew so abundantly they were a nuisance. Shortly before Christmas a delegation of young men of the community drove to this ranch and brought back wagonloads of trees for all the families and the two big trees for the churches.

Our Christmas tree was never decorated by the children and parents together, as is the custom in many families now, nor was the tree ever put up weeks before Christmas. The time was the evening of December 24. In the afternoon the room was closed off, and one of our parents and some of the older children decorated the tree and put on the candles. We were told that the *Weihnachtsmann,* the "Christmas man" or Santa Claus, would come and bring the presents that evening, but he never appeared to us. Then after supper, when all was ready, one of the parents rang a little bell and announced that the *Weihnachtsmann* had come and had brought presents for us. Sometimes we heard the old fellow walk across the front porch on his way out.

Now the long-awaited moment had come, and the family walked into the Christmas room together to see the brightly lighted and decorated tree and the gifts and goodies. The presents were not wrapped at all. They stood or lay under the tree in full view of everybody, but before we could touch the gifts, my mother had us stand and sing "Der schönste Baum" ("The Fairest Tree"):

> Der Christbaum ist der schönste Baum,
> Den wir auf Erden kennen.
> Im Garten klein, im engsten Raum,
> Wie lieblich blüht der Wunderbaum,
> Wenn seine Blümlein brennen,
> Wenn seine Blümlein brennen,
> Ja brennen.
>
> *(Psalter und Harfe,* 21)

> (The Christ-tree is the fairest tree,
> That we on earth can know.
> In smallest rooms, our eyes can see
> How lovely blooms the wondrous tree
> With its fiery blossoms glowing,
> With its fiery blossoms glowing,
> Yes glowing.)

When the song was done, we children received our toys and presents. We also took a quick look at the bench on which were boxes or plates filled with candy, cookies, oranges, and apples. Strange as it may seem now, apples and oranges were a special Christmas treat for us, not a regular daily food item. The adults and parents shared in the goodies, but there was no exchanging of presents among grown-ups.

In my family, we heard nothing of hanging up stockings by the chimney. We had enough long stockings for boys and girls alike, but we did not have a fireplace. All the stories about Christmas stockings and jolly old St. Nick landing his sleigh and reindeer on the roof and sliding down the chimney with presents simply did not exist in our world.

Somehow our *Weihnachtsmann* sneaked into the house while we were eating supper and trudged off again before we finished eating. He was unquestionably a pedestrian. Or he may have had a horse tied to a gate post, but we kids never found any evidence of this. Some of the older boys, who had lost faith in the elusive Santa Claus, even dared to repeat jeering verses about him, like:

> Ich bin klein, du bist gross;
> Der Weihnachtsmann hat ein Loch in der Hos'.
>
> (I am small, you are big;
> Santa Claus has a hole in his pants.)

In my mother's family there was some talk of the Christ Child (*das Christkindlein*) bringing the presents. This tradition was brought along by my grandfather Anton Willmann, who was a Catholic from Silesia. The custom seems to have ended for him after he became a Methodist and settled among Protestants in Mason County.

We never had a crèche, or manger scene, such as are common in Catholic families of Europe and more recently also in many American homes. Nor was there any talk about the twelve nights of Christmas, so we could not sing "On the first day of Christmas, my truelove gave to me." We did know and keep the old German custom of "Second Christmas" on December 26, which was set aside for visiting among friends and relatives. We had visitors in our home or we drove in our hack and buggy to spend the day visiting.

Fireworks did not play as big a role with us as they did in some German communities. We did have our firecrackers, both the larger kind, which could almost blow off your fingers if they exploded before you got rid of them, and the small ones that came in packets of several dozen little crackers with intertwined fuses. We never used matches to light the fuses; we used a shovelful of live coals. We also had Roman candles, sky rockets, and sparklers. What we did not have were the mighty dynamite blasts of the New Braunfels Germans. Perhaps the mild Methodists looked with disfavor on these earth-shaking explosions, in which large rocks and even anvils were blown up with dynamite.

On New Year's Eve, the young people held Watchnight parties and services at one of the churches. Some of the boys and girls had dates, and some of the others paired off during the early part of the evening when we had programs, singing, and parlor games. As midnight approached, we assembled for religious services until the New Year arrived. After the services, there was some shooting of fireworks, and then everybody went home.

Good Friday and Easter activities were not as elaborate as our Christmas celebrations. The religious element was again kept in the foreground, beginning with the somber Good Friday (*Karfreitag*) services and ending with the joyous Easter morning celebration, both held in the church. The church bell seemed to ring out more clearly and joyously on Easter Day than on other occasions, and the people could rejoice, "Christ ist erstanden" ("Christ is risen").

Like many of our Christmas customs, the Easter rabbit and the colored eggs came from Germany. However, our parents were smart enough not to try to sell us on the idea of an egg-laying rabbit. Even the kids knew too much about rabbits and birds to accept this folklore, no matter how German it might be. Our Easter rabbit had a much easier time of it. He simply dyed the hard-boiled eggs and put them into flowery nests (*Osternester*) that we prepared for him. I don't remember how much faith the little kids had in the rabbit's activities, but among adults he was a questionable character, so they referred to an unreliable person as an *Osterhase* (an "Easter rabbit").

On the Saturday before Easter we children always went on a flower-hunting expedition. We took a child's wagon and some baskets or buckets and went out to the pasture and fields to gather flowers and fresh grass for our Easter nests. We fixed the nests on the front porch, where the Easter rabbit could easily find them and fill them with gay-colored eggs. Naturally we children never had any part in the egg dyeing; this was the Easter rabbit's job. The day after Easter was "Second Easter" (*Zweite Ostern*) for us. Like "Second Christmas" this was a holiday, and most of the people spent the day visiting friends and relatives.

None of the other holidays played as big a role as Chirstmas and Easter. To be sure, we did celebrate most of the typical American holidays, but they were less prominent in the lives of the children. We celebrated Thanksgiving Day, calling it *Danksagungstag* in German (literally, "Thanks-saying-day"). Although this holiday is as American as baseball, hot dogs, and apple pie, Germans also have an old tradition of a *Danktag* ("day of thanks") and an *Erntefest* ("harvest festival"). Germans sing "Nun, danket alle Gott," just as we sing in translation "Now, Thank We All Our God." Thus the religious element of Thanksgiving was natural for my family. What was new at first was the American stuffed-turkey, cranberry-sauce, and pumpkin-pie dinner, which was accepted only slowly.

Other Anglo-American special days were also adopted and soon became important to the German-Texas communities. Among these were the Confederate reunions, Independence Day, Halloween, and Valentine Day, all in the American style. The patriotic songs and traditions associated with the reunions and Independence Day came to us primarily in English, but we also learned German versions, and some of the church songbooks had "The Star-Spangled Banner" ("Das Sternenbanner") and "My Country, 'Tis of Thee" ("Amerika") in German.

Our social life was scanty and simple, but we did have occasional get-togethers at which we played various games. The American play party came to our community and provided us with entertainment. Strictly Anglo, it was well known throughout the country. In our rural area, it was better accepted than square dancing, which was frowned on, no matter how square it was. The words and music of the games were easy to learn, and the promenading and rhythmic skipping around were much simpler than folk dancing. The play parties or socials were given by various families, including ours, and all the young people of the community came. The more active games were played outdoors, but they could also be played in a large room. Our favorites were: musical chairs, fruit basket turn over, drop the handkerchief, wink 'em, blind man's buff, three deep, London bridge is falling down, marching round the levee, and skip to my Lou. The latter is a simple game. Partners are chosen, and the couples stand in a circle. The action and singing start when the boy without a partner begins to sing and skip around. He goes to someone's girl partner and "steals" the girl while he and the group of players sing "I'll get me a partner, skip to my Lou," etc. Then he and his new partner skip away, and the boy who lost his partner starts off on his search, while he leads the singing of "I've lost my partner, what'll I do," etc., or "Stole my partner, skip to my Lou," etc., or "I'll get another one, prettier than you," etc. And so it goes on from one player to another, and various verses or improvisations are sung.

In playing "marching round the levee," the players form a circle, join hands, and, while one boy stays in the circle, march around singing:

> We're marching round the levee, (*repeat twice*)
> For we have gained today.

Then the promenaders stop, grasp hands, raise their arms to make windows, and sing "Go in and out the window," while the boy in the center goes in and out under the arched arms in the circle. While the third stanza is sung, "I measure my love to show you," he chooses a partner, faces her, holds her hands, and the two players swing their hands together. Then while the crowd sings "I kneel because I love you," the boy kneels before the girl. After he gets up, the players sing "Farewell, I hate to leave you," and the girl leaves the boy and goes into the circle, and the whole thing is repeated.

The American custom of sending cards for most of the special days soon caught on in the German-Texas communities. To be sure, my youth came and went before the present-day avalanche of Christmas cards, greeting cards, birthday cards, get-well cards, sympathy cards, Halloween cards, comic cards, graduation cards, and Easter cards, but the card game had already started good and proper. Our cards were old-fashioned picture postcards. On the back side there was space for a one-cent stamp and for the name and address, plus a section for "correspondence," "communication," or "messages."

The pictures on the old cards have a charming nineteenth-century flavor. The colorful roses, forget-me-nots, birds, and human hands remind me of the friendship cards discussed below. I found one card showing a blue-coated, pedestrian Santa with a basket and a green bag, both filled with toys. This Santa is no "jolly old elf"; he looks glum, like his European prototype St. Nicholas, but apparently he is kind to the children.

The Thanksgiving Day cards show over-size, puffed-up turkeys pursuing frightened children. The Easter cards portray children, eggs, chicks, lambs, and Easter lilies, in addition to an occasional rabbit. One valentine card from 1910 depicts a little boy in blue, eating red stick candy. The inscription reads "If you'll be mine, I'll tell you true, / I'll give my candy all to you."

In addition to the valentines with love messages, there were also some anonymous, vinegar valentines, exchanged among boys and men. Some were harmless and humorous, but others were taken seriously and called forth much teasing. The expression "to get a valentine" often had the connotation among boys and men of getting a derogatory epistle. I remember once a bald-headed uncle of mine got a real lulu of a valentine, depicting an old, bald-pated codger in a silly pose. This uncle, being suspicious by nature, immediately decided who had played the prank on him. He sent the same valentine to the boy whom he suspected, adding further disparaging embellishments. When this innocent boy received the thing, he in turn accused some other school kid and sent him the infamous "billet-doux" with further nasty additions.

One interesting and lovely practice was the custom of giving friendship cards. These little cards were exchanged among all schoolchildren, even among parents, uncles, aunts, teachers, and preachers. The back section was a small, white card with the name of the giver printed on the front. Attached to one end and covering the name were flowery and lacy overlays (*Stammbuchblümchen* in German), that could be raised up so that you could read the name of the giver.

Certain themes appear again and again on these gay-colored overlays, both in the floral designs and in the sentiments of the messages. The verses are sweet and precious, like the following:

> Of all that is near, you are the nearest;
> Of all that is dear, you are the dearest.

> May flowerets of love
> Around thee be twined,
> And the sunshine of peace
> Shed its joys o'er thy mind.

Some cards have a slight touch of humor in their message: "I wish I could catch you," and "To my birdie."

Another interesting custom was the writing of verses in memory books or albums (*Stammbücher*). Here are a few prize specimens:

> Your album is a golden spot
> To write in it: "Forget me not."

Some love one, some love two;
I love one, and that is you.

When you get old and cannot see,
Put on your specs and think of me.

May you be happy each day of your life,
Get a good husband and make a good wife.

In a church-oriented community like Plehweville it was only natural that some books also contained religious and other-worldly verses:

May you and I in heaven meet
And cast our crowns at Jesus' feet.

Also a number of German verses occur in these memory books, for example:

Dem kleinen Veilchen gleich,
Das im Verborgnen blüht,
Sei immer fromm und gut,
Auch wenn dich niemand sieht.

(Like a little violet,
That blooms in secrecy,
Be pious and be good,
Though unseen you may be.)

The custom of giving a shivaree, a mock serenade for newly-weds after a big home wedding, was well known in the German Texas Hill Country. We called a shivaree a *Katzenmusik* (literally, "cat's music"; this means "caterwauling" which is itself derived from the German word *Kater*, "tomcat," plus *waul*, "wail"). The custom of a shivaree is related to the old German *Polterabend*, a noisy, wedding-eve party, during which broken dishes and old pots and pans are thrown against the front door until the betrothed appear and serve refreshments.

A Texas-style shivaree was, however, something else again and much more boisterous. The men and boys came on horseback, riding like wild cowboys, shouting, yelling, dragging tin cans, beating on buckets and washtubs, ringing cowbells, and blowing horns. They usually made a number of mad dashes around the house, scaring the dogs so that they joined in the din with their barking. It was enough to stampede even docile milch cows and tame horses.

Proverbs, *Sprichwörter* in German, were an ever-ready source of folk wisdom and a vital part of our cultural heritage. These sayings, constantly on the lips of parents and elderly people, helped preserve a traditional life-style that was basically conservative. Here are a few of the many proverbs most commonly quoted and memorized during my childhood:

> *Der Klügste gibt nach.*
> (The wisest one gives in.)

> *Frisch begonnen ist halb gewonnen.*
> (Well begun is half done.)

> *Hunger ist der beste Koch.*
> (Hunger is the best cook.)

> *Viele Hände machen schnell ein Ende.*
> (Many hands will finish a job quickly.)

> *Wenn die Maus satt ist, schmeckt das Mehl bitter.*
> (When the mouse is full, flour will taste bitter.)

> *Wer andern eine Grube gräbt, fällt selbst hinein.*
> (He who digs a pit to trap others will fall in himself.)

In our community, the people put more emphasis on the role of godparents (*Paten* or *Taufzeugen*) than is customary now, and there was something of a special relationship between godparent and godchild. I remember that my godmother, Mrs. Adolph Kothmann, née Lydia Hoerster, often gave me presents while I was a child.

We had several other customs that were typical of the Texas-German group. Whenever we met anybody we knew or took leave from somebody, we went through a lot of handshaking ceremony. We called this *die Hände schütteln*, but a more appropriate German expression would be *jemandem die Hand geben* ("to give somebody your hand"), an expression of real warmth and cordiality, which carries no obligation to shake up some gentle soul with a violent handshake. I met a fellow once, however, who crushed your hand with his iron grip and all but shook your arm loose at the shoulder.

People usually said, "Guten Tag, wie geht's bei euch?" ("Good day, how are you all?"), or perhaps with a slight dig at the complainers, who mistook a greeting for an inquiry about their health, "Sonst geht's gut?" ("Otherwise is everything going well?"). The German expression *Wie geht's* means literally "How goes it?" but the verb *gehen* also means "to walk," so you were not only saying "How goes it?" but also "How do you walk?" This sometimes called forth the facetious reply "Auf zwei Beinen, wie einer Gans" ("On two legs, like a goose").

When we were small children, our parents, especially Father, bounced us on their knees or let us ride on a foot while they sang or recited children's riding songs similar to the English ditty "This Is the Way the Lady Rides." At the end of each song they pretended to drop us, as though we were falling off the horse. Here is my favorite riding verse:

> Wenn die Kinder kleine sein,
> Reiten sie auf Stöckelein;
> Wenn sie grösser werden,
> Reiten sie auf Pferden.
> Dann geht das Pferdchen tripp und trab,
> Und schmeisst den kleinen Reiter ab.
> Plumps! da liegt er unten.
>
> (When the kids are small and wee,
> A stickhorse will their horsie be;
> When they're big and stronger,
> They'll ride their horses longer,
> Then the horse goes pit-a-pat
> And throws the rider tit for tat.
> Bump! he hits the bottom.)

Another popular riding ditty was:

> Hopp, hopp, hopp!
> Pferdchen, lauf Galopp,
> Über Stock und über Steinchen,
> Pferdchen, brich dir nur kein Beinchen!
> Hopp, hopp, hopp, hopp, hopp!
> Pferdchen, lauf Galopp!
>
> (Trot, trot, trot!
> Horsie, run a lot,

Over sticks and over stonies,
Do not fall and break your bonies.
Trot, trot, trot, trot, trot!
Horsie, run a lot!)

We also had our little verses similar to the English rhyme "Patty cake, patty cake, baker's man." As with the English poem, our parents taught us to pat our hands while we sang or said:

Backe, backe Kuchen!
Der Bäcker hat gerufen:
Wer will guten Kuchen backen,
Der muss haben sieben Sachen:
Eier und Schmalz, Zucker und Salz,
Milch und Mehl,
Safran macht den Kuchen gehl [gelb].
Schieb in den Ofen 'nein.

(Baking, baking, cookie!
The baker man is calling:
Who will bake a tasty cake,
Seven things he has to take:
Eggs and lard, sugar and salt,
Milk and flour,
Saffron makes the cake turn yellow.
Shove it through the oven door.)

A lovely German custom that we used when a child got hurt was to kiss and blow on the sore spot and say or sing:

Heile, heile, Segen,
Drei Tage Regen;
Drei Tage Dreck,
Und jetzt ist alles weg.

(Healing, healing, blessing,
Three days of rain;
Three days of mud,
And now there's no more pain.)

The belief that good and talented children will die early or young, that is to say, that the Lord will take away the good little children to Himself, was commonly held. When I was still very small, my mother and my older sisters taught me to sing many songs like "Rock-a-bye, Baby" in English and my mother's favorite song "Jesus, Heiland meiner Seele" ("Jesus, Lover of my Soul"), all six stanzas in German. I enjoyed singing, and I sang at the drop of a pin. When Aunt Emma, Uncle Peter Jordan's wife, heard me sing such German church songs, she said to my mother in German, "You won't keep him long; the Good Lord will take him from you." Of course, Aunt Emma was wrong. And if she had heard me sing after I grew up, she surely would have recanted.

We did not have any special birthday celebrations for the children, but we always received a round of congratulations. After we got our telephone, my father never failed to call up his brothers and sisters to congratulate them on their *Geburtstag*. Our parents always urged us to get up early and be especially good on our birthdays. We were told that our actions on this day would determine our behavior for a whole year.

Family reunions began as birthday celebrations for the early German settlers after they had acquired large clans of children and grandchildren. In my family, Grandmother Willmann's birthday was the occasion for these gatherings. She had thirteen children of her own, and they all came with their large families, the whole *Sippschaft* ("clan"), adding up to a crowd of well over a hundred hungry relatives. They came not only from Mason County but also from Gillespie, Bexar, and Comal counties. The entire house, porch, and yard, in fact the whole farmstead, were filled with people and horses and hacks. It was a jolly occasion for the kids, but Grandmother probably aged by several years each time. The family reunions have continued to the present day and have multiplied and grown in magnitude. Great gatherings are held by many of the early families. One outgrowth of the continuing family ties that the reunions foster has been a number of family histories written about the pioneer German families.

We had a number of folkloric practices and home remedies. Our best cure for a sore throat was to sip heated honey mixed with vinegar, but my father preferred peppermint tablets. Tobacco juice or a "chaw" of freshly chewed tobacco was applied to insect stings and bites, or, if that wasn't available, coal oil was applied and had the same results. A harmless remedy for rheumatism was to steal a small white potato and carry it in your pocket until it got wrinkled and dried. If this pet potato rotted instead of drying, the results were unfavorable. A strange practice was to treat a thorn or splinter as well as the wound it inflicted. I remember seeing my mother place the extracted thorn or splinter in hot lard and turpentine and treat it along with the wound.

And there was also the asafetida treatment for the prevention of sickness. Whenever a contagious disease broke out among the children, say, diphtheria, Mother hung a bag of asafetida around our necks. Even though we wore this vile-smelling locket under our shirts and blouses, we still got the full benefit of its odor, and so did our friends. Only those people who have smelled this infernal substance at a distance of ten feet can understand why asafetida is called *Teufelsdreck* ("devil's dirt") in German. If you happen to smell it at a distance of two feet, you will surely use a different four-letter English word that is semantically related to *dirt* and that will describe the vile product better. Interestingly, asafetida was quite effective in preventing the spread of disease germs. Because of the stench tied around your neck, your friends, including those who were carriers of germs, kept at such a distance from you that you were never properly exposed to other people's germs.

Dropping a piece of silverware, especially a fork, was a sure sign that we would have visitors or company. I think there must have been a lot of fork dropping at our place just before "Second Christmas" and "Second Easter" and before the summer vacations, for our relatives descended upon us in swarms. When your ears began to ring, you had a sure sign that somebody was talking about you, and you hoped it was a friend saying something good.

Country people have always lived close to nature, so there is a great mass of folklore about natural phenomena. Some of the sayings and beliefs are as old as the hills. There are a number of interesting weather signs, as this German verse suggests:

> Abendrot, gut Wetter droht;
> Morgenrot, schlecht Wetter droht.
>
> (Evening red, good weather ahead.;
> Morning red, bad weather ahead.)

This same weather prediction is also found in several English versions.

The moon also prophesies the weather. When the horns of the new moon both point upward, the moon will hold up the water and keep it from falling. When there is enough moisture in the air, the moon will have a halo. We called this halo a *Hof* (a "yard" or "court-yard"), and it meant rain in three days. Also a round, fat, full moon was a rain sign, but I don't remember whether positive or negative. And we always heard that a dry winter was in store if the first norther blew in dry and dusty.

We also heard all the familiar moon signs about times for planting seeds, setting out plants, and cutting fence posts. My father said we should cut mesquite posts when the moon was waning. Some people also believed they should brand calves when the moon wanes to keep the brands from growing too big. There were several other tokens by which Mother Nature let us know some of her secrets. My father always said that a good crop of white thistles in the field in spring meant an abundant corn crop in summer.

Water witching has a long tradition in both Anglo and German folklore. Well witchers are called *Brunnenschmöker* ("well hunters") in some German-Texas settlements, and many people would stake their eternal salvation on the reliability of the forked sticks. I have known some people who claimed to have such well-trained divining rods or forked sticks that they could easily find the spots where underground water was available. Not only that; these sticks knew just how deep you had to drill to hit the water level. They twitched or nodded their heads to indicate how many feet you had to dig or drill.

There were other folkloric practices that enjoyed varying degrees of credibility. Some people believed they could make their fruit trees more productive by driving rusty nails into the trunks. I remember that once we subjected a pear tree to this abuse. The tree did not die prematurely, but I don't remember that it got more productive either.

The most spurious bit of folkloric practice is what we called faith healing but what was really more like magic spells. It is very difficult to get any faithful believer to divulge all he knows about this method of exorcising worms and evil spirits. I think the practitioners always detect the skeptic in me and promptly clam up when I begin to ask questions. I suppose if I were to express a great desire to practice this medical and spiritual hoax, I might find somebody to initiate me into the brotherhood. But no, I don't mean brotherhood! The mysteries can be revealed only by a woman to a man or by a man to a woman.

Even some of the initiates seem to have a guilty conscience about this half-sinful practice. You see, you have to call upon the Holy Trinity to rid yourself or your cattle of worms and evil spirits. On top of that you have to indulge in all manner of hocus-pocus and mumbo-jumbo, and you must not forget to lay three sticks or matches in a triangular position to represent the Holy Trinity.

The exorcising of worms by some charm (*Wurmsegen* in German) is a practice that goes back to ancient times, even to the pre-Christian era and *Wodan* worship. There are a number of such charms (*Segenssprüche* in German), and they are some of the oldest documents of written Old High German. It is interesting, indeed, to see them crop up even now in the German Belt of Texas, three thousand miles from the place of their origin and thousands of years later.

Some rural people were inveterate pranksters, and many of the tricks provided great entertainment for the country kids. Every boy had to be subjected to a snipe hunt. The novice was stationed beside some bushes or trees, as far away from home as possible, on a dark night. He was supposed to hold open a tow sack to catch the snipes. The conspirators went along to chase the snipes out of the underbrush. They put on a big show of yelling and beating the bushes for some time, but then they withdrew silently and sneaked home, leaving the greenhorn all alone in the spooky woods. Sometimes the prank backfired on the conspirators when a smart kid would lead the pranksters to believe that he was a greenhorn. After the big boys left him holding the bag and went off to chase the snipes, the smart kid ran home and had the last laugh. *Wer zuletzt lacht, lacht am besten* ("He who laughs last laughs best").

Spooks and ghosts did not bother us, but there were several families that had frequent encounters and believed their houses were haunted. They said "Es spukt bei uns" ("There are spooks in our house"), and they were right. The pranksters managed to rattle chains and make weird sounds so realistically by fastening a string to a window, stretching it tight, and rubbing it with rosin, that the victims were thoroughly convinced.

We knew nothing about "tricks or treats," but we indulged heavily in Halloween pranks. Some of these were group projects and caused much trouble and vexation for the victims. It required the combined efforts of several boys to hoist a buggy to the roof of a shed or barn, to remove all the wheels from a wagon or a hack, to over-turn an outhouse or transport it to the front yard or to the pasture, to haul off or hide gates, saddles, and harnesses, or even to pull a vehicle to the sandy crossing of a creek. A rather resourceful prank was tying a tame cow to the bell rope in a church or a school. This prank usually rousted up and infuriated the principal or the preacher, as the case might be, to the great amusement of the pranksters.

In general, there was not as much fun and play among the Methodists as among other German settlers, but there were, never-theless, many pleasant activities that provided entertainment and enriched their lives. Christmas, Easter, children's songs and verses, church programs, play parties, games, picnics, cards, albums, shiva-rees, and family reunions provided pleasant relief from the heavy work of everyday life.

8

Stopping and Shopping in Town

My father was not exactly the shopping kind of man; he was more the stopping kind. That is to say, he enjoyed walking along on the high sidewalks of Mason and into the stores and talking with the merchants and friends from the country. When I was still a small boy, I usually tagged along and listened to the rural talk about the weather, the rain, the drought, the crops, the pastures, the grass, the cows, and the calves they had dropped lately. These were noncontroversial topics, and the men nodded their Stetson-covered heads in agreement. In politics there was an occasional argument, but my father and his rural cronies usually agreed. They would vote for Teddy Roosevelt for president, even if he ran on the Purple Cow ticket instead of the Bull Moose Party, and they would vote for P. C. Baird for sheriff, even if he had nothing but a water pistol instead of his big six-shooter.

The city of Mason has one of the largest courthouse squares in the state of Texas, if not in the entire United States. The sidewalks around the square were ideal for unscheduled meetings and chatting because they were built up high and the people could stand in the shade on the covered sidewalks above the street level. There were some special advantages to the high sidewalks, at least in the pioneer days. The people stood as tall on the sidewalks as the men on horseback stood in their stirrups. If it ever came to a shooting scrape, the pedestrians were not at a great disadvantage but could hold their own in any six-shooter confrontations. There was, however, one sidewalk danger totally unrelated to the height of the walks: the whittling and spitting bench. You always passed this area near the Mason Drug Store at your own risk. Mason needed a Carrie Nation who would have taken her ax and chopped down the sitters' and spitters' bench. But that would not have been altogether for the good either, because then there would not have been any place outside the courthouse yard for telling the tall tales that emerged from the bench along with the tobacco juice.

One of the cleaner tall tales heard on the whittle-spittle bench concerns a cattle drive. According to the story, the cook on the chuck wagon got tired of feeding a big bunch of complaining cowboys on the long drive. He quit and went back to his cow pony. Nobody was ready to do the cooking. Finally, in desperation, one of the men agreed to take over the job, but he warned, "Iff'n any o' yo goldurned cowpokes says one complaining word, I'll quit, and that son-of-a-gun has to take over the cooking." The first breakfast turned out fairly well because anybody can fry salt bacon and corn pone and cook camp coffee, so nobody said a word. However, for supper the in-experienced cook produced an almost inedible hash, something that tasted like dog food. The leader of the complaining cowboys took a bite or two, made a terrible face, and said: "Dad-blame-it, consarn-it, confound-it, ———! That is the worst—I meant to say, that is the best food I ever et." This was a close call, and there never was heard another discouraging word.

In the earlier days, before the automobile era, the eighteen-mile round-trip shopping expedition from our ranch to town usually took a full day. The roads were rough and sandy and only partly graded, so we drove slowly. On the country road from our house to the big road we had to open and close four gates and cross some ten or more diverter dams built across the road to drain off the water. These things were called "damn Dutchman's dumps" by the less respectful Anglos. They were harmless to wagons, hacks, and buggies, but years later, when a person rode in the backseat of a Model T Ford, he would be pitched up high and almost knocked out going over these dumps at thirty miles an hour.

Traveling by buggy, hack, or wagon was not always as safe as we might think now. The columns of the *Mason County News* gave many accounts of accidents with vehicles and horses: "Ab Smart had a runaway Saturday, resulting in a loss of peeling to him and two other boy companions, besides a torn up buggy and a spoiled team" (January 12, 1912. Reprinted in 1952). "Wm. Houy of Castell was badly hurt last week when he fell from his loaded wagon, and the wheel passed over his head" (January 9, 1903. Reprinted in 1953).

When we drove to town, we often stopped along the way so my father could talk leisurely with a friend or an acquaintance beside the road. These roadside chats were what my father missed most after we acquired our car. On one occasion we saw a farmer piling up a small mountain of rocks near his field beside the road. My father stopped and talked with the man, who, like many others, was displeased with President Wilson because he had let the country go to war shortly after he had been elected on a ticket that proclaimed, "He kept us out of war." My father asked this man, "Say, what are you doing there? Are you building a monument to President Wilson?" The farmer answered, "Yes, that's right, but I wish I had him underneath."

Only rarely did our family journey together to Mason. On one memorable occasion, however, the whole family advanced *en masse* to the county capital. It was a cavalcade of thirteen people (our immediate family plus my first brother-in-law), two buggies, one hack, one gig, a few horseback riders, and nine or ten horses. The whole *Sippschaft* ("clan") drove to town to have a family portrait made. That sort of mass movement into a studio would unnerve any modern photographer, but in those days this was quite normal.

I can still hear the big family stalk up the creaky wooden stairs and into the bleak studio. These group pictures usually turned out grim and disastrous, but we got through the ordeal without any major casualty, and each of us put on the appropriate, nineteenth-century, rural-Gothic pose. There was a lot of staring and juggling around with lights, reflectors, and camera. Several times the agile photographer ducked under the ominous black cloth hung over the back of the large camera. Finally he crawled out, stood up by the side, and, adjusting a rubber bulb in his hand, admonished us to stand still. We stood like statues and stared resolutely at the black box until something clicked. Just when we thought we could relax, he went through the whole ceremony again. It was like getting married twice in one day.

On the day of the photography expedition we had many other things to do and many stores to visit. For the most part, the men went their way and the women did their shopping. It was customary among Texans for the husbands to hold the money purse, and so it was in our family, but things were beginning to change, and my mother had learned to do some of the family shopping herself when she came to town. As the family scattered all over the large square and to various stores, my father went up the street to buy a hat. As he proceeded toward Hofmann's Dry Goods Company, accompanied by my brother Milton and me, he stopped often for sidewalk chats, but we finally arrived at the dry-goods establishment. We were greeted by Wilhelm Hofmann, the owner. He said in a friendly tone of voice: "Na, wie geht's denn immer noch bei dir, Daniel? Ist aber schön, dass du dich mal wieder sehen lässt" ("Well how are you by now, Daniel? It's good that you let us see you again"). Then we all shook hands, including us kids. After a fifteen-minute conversation, Herr Hofmann said, "Na also, was soll's heute sein?" ("Now then, what will you have today?"), and my father replied that he needed a hat to replace his old Stetson. All the new hats looked alike, so Father tried them on for size. "Der Hut sitzt wie angeschossen, Daniel, und ist von allerbester Qualität" ("The hat fits as if it had been shot on, Daniel, and it is of the very best quality"), said Herr Hofmann. Father took it and paid cash. This would now be his Sunday hat, and the old one would be demoted to everyday use, no matter how hot and heavy it was.

Father did not dare roll or push up the brim at the sides as modern pickup-truck and rodeo cowboys do. Nor did he crease the fine crown of the hat into an odd shape. He just let his friend Wilhelm give the crown a gentle crease; then he wore the hat as upright as his character, and it was becoming to him. Oh, he may have looked a bit Amish, but one thing is sure: he never looked like a donkey with his ears pinned back. He respected his Stetson hats and he knew that gentleman cattle breeders take off their hats at home, in restaurants, and in church. Father really needed a new pair of Sunday shoes, the kind with broad, boxy toes and hooks for the laces, but he would put off buying the shoes until later. Instead, he went on down to the bootmaker's shop and bought some black Shinola shoe polish, with which my mother could polish his old shoes.

The prosperous Swedish bootmaker, Oscar Seaquist, had a shop on the north side of the square. He became so affluent that he bought the most pretentious stone residence in Mason, the Reynolds home. Everybody who was anybody in Mason County, including my father and my brothers, wore boots made to order by Mr. Seaquist. We usually went by this shop even when we had no business to transact. It was fun to watch the master shoemaker at work, and the fresh leather smell of the shop was almost as pungent as the odors in the saddle shops further down the square.

In the early 1900's, cattle raisers and horsemen could find saddle and leather shops as easily as modern car buffs can find garages and filling stations. Henrich's Saddle Shop was built, owned, and operated by the Henrichs, first the father and then his son Ed Henrich. It was always worth your time to see these saddlers, if for no other reason than to smell the fragrant leather. These men made or sold not only plain and fancy saddles but also bullwhips and quirts, riding chaps, bridles, harnesses, horse collars, buggy whips, belts, spurs, stirrups, holsters, saddlebags, saddle blankets, halters, bridle reins, and other leather goods, as well as gloves and hemp rope.

There were several banks in town during the early part of the twentieth century, just as there are now. We patronized the Commercial Bank, Unincorporated. The president of the bank was Mrs. Anna Martin, a rich widow, storekeeper, and ranch operator from Hedwig's Hill. Together with her sons, she had bought a defunct bank and founded a new financial institution in 1901. The Commercial Bank was as solid as the square mile of granite making up the Enchanted Rock Mountain. Anybody could tell that there was lots of money in the vaults because the whole place had a strong smell of greenbacks, as prominent as Anna Martin's presence.

A regular business procedure at the bank was to get your bankbook balanced. You left your book at the bank during one visit and picked it up the next time. The bookkeepers recorded all the cancelled checks and handed the book back with the checks and deposit slips. "Das war klug von dir, Daniel, dass du die Blue Mountain Ränsch gekauft hast. Wenn du mehr Geld brauchst, kannst du es hier haben, so viel, wie du willst" ("That was smart of you, Daniel, that you bought the Blue Mountain ranch. If you need more money, you can have it here, as much as you wish"), said Anna Martin to my father when he picked up his bankbook. She had a keen eye for business, and she knew her customers.

There was another solid bank nearly two blocks down the square to the east, the German-American National Bank, where two Anglo Americans, Capps and White, and two German Texans, Geistweidt and Lemburg, stored your money. However, neither the words *German-American*, nor the designation *National Bank* could lure my family away from the Martins. Later a third bank, the First State Bank was established, but it soon merged with the First National Bank, the successor to the old German-American National Bank, which lost its name during or after World War I, when everything German was taboo and suspect. Fortunately, the bank did not suffer any losses during the anti-German prejudice, from which the town recovered only slowly.

Actually, the first Mason County bank was not in Mason but in Koocksville, a few miles to the northwest. There Wilhelm Koock kept the people's money safely, at first in his log house and after 1883 in the large hewn-stone building that served as a store, bank, and trading post. Upstairs was a meeting place for lodges, clubs, dances, and entertainment. Overhead was the lookout tower, useful in case of attacks by Indians or outlaws. If any commercial building in Mason County deserves restoration and preservation, it is the Koocksville store.

In the early days of the 1890's, Mason had an excellent German baker, my uncle Fritz Stengel. He baked the best bread and cakes in town, and he put on the fanciest decorations and icing, but in frontier Mason County all the rural people baked their own bread. So Uncle Fritz established a grocery store in place of the bakery, and he made his living chiefly from the sale of groceries. For a while he continued his fancy cake-trimming for the aesthetic pleasure he derived from it. But really, you could not make a living in a frontier town with any kind of art work, even if it was edible. *Die Kunst ist ein brotloses Gewerbe* ("Art is a breadless trade"), declares a German saying.

Uncle Fritz's grocery store was always rich in the most edifying fragrance in town. In those days grocery stores did not sell raw meats; consequently, they had no unpleasant odors of overage beef. There were only the sweet and pleasant smells of spices, sugar, apples, and coffee. Uncle Fritz was always glad when my parents loaded our hack or wagon with hundreds of pounds of staple groceries. In those days the country people bought wheat flour in white fifty-pound cotton sacks, sugar by the hundred pounds, and salt for curing meats, for table use, and for livestock in hundred-pound quantities. Prunes came in twenty-pound boxes, and coffee, in large barrels. Of course, we bought no meat, cheese, eggs, butter, vegetables, or fruit, except apples and oranges by the crate or barrel at Christmastime. We did not have to buy perishable goods, since we produced them ourselves. Sometimes we raised more than we could eat or process, in which case we sold the surplus to Hofmann's or Lemburg's stores or traded them for staple groceries.

The Brothers Lemburg knew we were good customers, whether on a given trip we were buying from them or selling our produce. They gave us kids candy every time our parents traded with them or paid off the big bill. We were the children of a developing ranchman, not a rich man, but one whose trade was important to the merchants, and they esteemed and respected us highly. After grocery shopping at Uncle Fritz's place, my mother and the girls went to Lemburg's store and selected some material for new dresses.

On one occasion I accompanied my father alone on a shopping trip to Mason. He took me along to open the gates and keep him company on the buggy ride to town. At such times we usually took along our lunch, but for some reason that day Mother forgot to put it into the buggy. Perhaps my father was quite willing to leave it behind. I suspect that for some time he had wanted to eat at the counter of the Mason chili joint. I had never tasted *chile con carne* before, so this meal eaten on the tall stools at the chili altar was a great surprise. Since we had to sit up very high, where no respectable lady would sit and eat, Papa chose a day when Mama was not along to try out the chili place. They served us big chunks of lean meat in a thin, red-hot chili sauce without beans. The chili emporium was nothing but a cheap, greasy-spoon joint, but I still have fond memories of the pieces of meat in the red chili sauce.

Speaking of driving to town reminds me of an apocryphal story my father used to tell. An old farmer, so the story goes, had to go to town to get a supply of axle grease, plowshares, horseshoes, a whetstone, a singletree, a halter, a horse collar, a pair of hames, coal oil, barb wire, and staples. He needed these supplies so urgently that he decided to go to town immediately. When his wife heard of his plans and saw him hitch up his horses to the wagon, she asked him to bring back some things for her. She wanted a spool of thread and a new needle. This was almost too much for the hard-working man to remember, and he objected because he knew he would forget these feminine things. So his wife began to drill the words into his head and made him repeat them after her: "A needle and a spool of thread! A needle and a spool of thread!" until he was ready to leave. He recited the words all the way to town: "A needle and a spool of thread."

When he arrived in town, still repeating the words, he tied his horses to a hitching post in front of Lemburg's store. Before he could forget his important mission, he rushed into the store and repeated his little ditty to the lady behind the counter: "A needle and a spool of thread." The clerk brought the desired articles with a smile. The farmer was happy and, with his mission accomplished, rushed out of the store, untied his horses, and drove off.

When he got home, his wife was standing in the doorway, awaiting his return. "Did you get my needle and the spool of thread?" she asked anxiously. The farmer, very proud of himself, replied: "Yes, I spoke those words to myself all the way to town and into the store. I got your needle and thread all right and came home without losing any time."

Said his wife when she saw his empty wagon: "But what about all those things you went to get from town?" "Oh, dadgum-it! This is the first time I thought about that. What will I do now?" "Well, I can sew up the worn seat of your britches with my needle and thread, and you can go back to town next week," said the understanding wife. The farmer's experience just goes to prove again the old German proverb *Was man nicht im Kopf hat, muss man in den Beinen haben* ("What you don't have in your head, you have to have in your legs").

Not far from Lemburg's store and Henrich's Saddle Shop on the east side of the square was Richard Grosse's lumberyard and hardware store. I relished the smell of all kinds of lumber in this place as much as I enjoyed the leather shops and Uncle Fritz's store. Herr Grosse wasn't an ordinary lumberyard proprietor; he was a German-trained builder, stonemason, and licensed architect. He wasn't exactly an early Gropius, Mies van der Rohe, or Frank Lloyd Wright, but he did draw the plans for the beautiful Mason Lutheran Church, and he designed and built several other prominent Mason County buildings, among them, the impressive Art and Hilda churches, the old grammar school, the Brandenburger stone houses and barns at Hilda, and, last but not least, the Reynolds-Seaquist home in Mason.

The three-story Seaquist home with its seventeen rooms, Victorian cupolas, gingerbread decorations, towers, chimneys, and wraparound porches resembles a European castle. It has recently been restored to its former splendor after several years of use as an apartment house. The building stands a few blocks north of the square. The artist and illustrator Buck Schiwetz found the building so striking that he sketched it, and the drawing was published in the well-known volume *Buck Schiwetz' Texas.* An excellent photograph of the same building also graces the pages of Drury B. Alexander's book, *Texas Homes of the Nineteenth Century.*

Throughout the entire German Belt of Texas we can still see many solid stone structures built by German-Texas stonemasons. These houses, barns, tank houses, wells, water reservoirs (tanks), smokehouses, schools, stores, and churches are a characteristic feature of the German settlements in Texas. You do not have to go far to see them in Mason; they stand all around you. Take a look at the Mason House on the northeast corner of the square, Henrich's Saddle Shop, the Koocksville store and well, and many other buildings in the town of Mason. Or go to the small German settlements and rural areas of Mason County and see the stone churches, the Hasse and the Otto Donop houses at Art, the old Zesch home near the Llano River, the stone barn on the Fritz Grote place, the old Eckert and Ellebracht homes, and many others. These structures were built for permanence, and, indeed, they have stood a long time.

There is one stone building on the south side of the square that we never visited, and that is the solid-rock jail. This prison is built so strong and secure because the earlier jail was not too safe. On some occasions, back in the 1870's, several cattle rustlers and horse thieves were removed by force and hanged on a post-oak tree, and there was always the danger of jail breaks. These lynchings and escapes saved a lot of court costs, but that is not what the people wanted, so the jail and courthouse were built solid as a rock.

The courthouse with its dome-like, turtle-neck tower stands in the center of the immense square and is now partly hidden in a grove of magnificent pecan trees. The building stands so low that it has to stretch its neck to look out above the trees, but that is not bad, because the trees are a wonderful asset to the square now that the original live-oak trees are gone. All the people enjoyed hearing the big clock strike the hours, and they set their watches by the mighty booms in the tower.

We made frequent visits to the courthouse, sometimes accompanied by Charles Bierschwale, who assisted my father with deeds and other legal matters. Mr. Bierschwale was a calm, level-headed counselor, and my father went to him frequently for advice. The courthouse also received many visits by country people because it had the only public flush toilets in town. Such modern conveniences were not common during the first three decades of the twentieth century. Running water was obtained from a well in the courthouse yard. A tall windmill and tank stood over this well during the many years when the city of Mason was an unincorporated town of windmills.

Blacksmith shops were as important, and almost as abundant, in pioneer days as garages and filling stations are now. Around the turn of the century, there were two such places on the square. On the east side was the Hermann and Louis Schmidt shop; the Schmidts were true to their name because *Schmidt* means "smith" in German. On the west side was Carl (Chas.) Guentert's place before he moved to the country near Grossville. The old Heinrich Doell shop was slightly off the square, behind the former Zork building. Then around 1909 Hugo Reichenau and Benno Keller set up their blacksmith shop. During my school days in Mason, only a few of these places were left.

Of course, the children in Mason, like the children in Longfellow's village in Maine, enjoyed seeing the sparks fly from the forge when the blacksmith pumped the bellows or when he beat on the red-hot iron. Modern "children coming home from school" in a big yellow bus are missing something thrilling when they can no longer stop and "look in at the open door," as Longfellow put it, and watch a blacksmith beat a hot bar of iron into the contours of a horseshoe or see the "mighty man" sharpen a plowshare by beating a keen edge on it. In the good old days you not only saw the blacksmith, but you also heard the clarion sound of his steel hammer pounding mightily upon the hot iron held with tongs on a solid-steel anvil. The loud, clanging sound pierced the air and could easily be heard across the entire square, no matter how large the town might be.

The country people made many visits to the blacksmith shops

because the blacksmith could take a rickety buggy or wagon wheel with loose spokes and a rattling rim and make it new again. Most of these smiths were also good carpenters and excellent wheelwrights, as well as metal craftsmen. If need be, they could completely rebuild a wagon wheel or the whole wagon, for that matter. Ready-made parts were not easy to obtain, so the blacksmiths built their own from scratch. It was fun to watch one of these craftsmen take off a loose rim, reduce its circumference, and put the rim back on the wooden wheel while the iron was still hot. Then he immersed the wheel and rim in water until the metal cooled and contracted. After this treatment, the rim fit as tight as a Stetson hat on a ranchman's head.

Not only did the blacksmiths tighten loose rims on wheels and shape iron horseshoes, they also shoed horses. Most ranchmen did this work at home, unless they had a horse that was ticklish about his feet. Problem horses were brought to town for a shoe fitting. The blacksmiths knew these horses by name and hated to see them come. Of course, the blacksmiths also had some easygoing customers, the tame city horses that pulled the buggies and surreys of the ladies in town and the delivery wagons of the merchants.

The coming of automobiles, trucks, and tractors after 1910 caused the rapid decline of the blacksmith shops. Soon there were more garages than smithies. There were Kensing's Garage on the square and the Star Garage on my way to school. In fact, the latter was near the home of the Otto Donops, with whom I stayed during my high-school days in Mason. The Donops used to be our neighbors on the Willow Creek, but they had moved to Mason after their retirement from farm and ranch work. Now Mr. Donop spent his spare time playing dominoes, while I slipped off to watch the mechanics at the automobile repair shop.

On the west side, the Star Garage had an elongated lean-to that housed the Odeon movie theater. This was the first picture-show house in Mason. Its proximity to the garage lent a sort of respectability to the theater and its silent movies and player piano. The affluent and more respectable people began to acquire cars, and the cars brought these people to the garage and, incidentally, also to the movies. The garage was about as good a hangout for school boys during my days in Mason High School as the early Mason blacksmith shops or Longfellow's smithy had been for school children earlier. We could see the mechanics take apart those old, high-slung vehicles and spread out the hundreds of parts all over the greasy floor, and then we could watch them put the parts back together again. The mechanics were not factory-trained; they were mostly self-educated. One thing is sure, though: they were mostly honest men and they did not gyp anyone. The customers paid only for what they got, and if the mechanics did not succeed in their first efforts, they did the job over without charging a second or third time.

There is some evidence that the first car owners had their share of trouble and then some. The *Mason County News* of August 13, 1909, reported as follows: "Wednesday was a bad day for autos, as there were three of Mason's four put out of order." The worst and funniest of the early-day accidents happened some fifteen years later in August, 1924. The paper described the event as follows:

On last Sunday night Otto Brockman had quite an exciting experience with a Ford car when he cranked it without the emergency brake being on. When the motor started, the car started, and Mr. Brockman, in attempting to hold the car with his foot against the front of the car, got in bad when his foot slipped between the spring and axle, and the car continued forward, throwing Mr. Brockman down and passing over him and dragging him off the bank into Comanche Creek. He attracted the attention of a number of people in that part of town with his yelling, and when assistance arrived, it was necessary that the spring be disconnected from the car before Mr. Brockman's leg could be gotten out.

There was one pint-sized German mechanic who must have come straight from the old country during the early age of automobiles in Mason. He was a good mechanic, but he was one of the windiest braggadocios I ever met anywhere. To hear him talk you would think that he could assemble the *Graf Zeppelin* airship single-handedly. When he did not know the English word for some of the parts he removed from the car, he simply translated the German words into English in his own peculiar, literal fashion, or he coined new words. This was a part of his genius. Many people are bilingual in everyday, simple conversation, but only a few can discuss technical matters in more than one language. The little German too had his problems in this respect. When there was something wrong with the carburetor, he promptly fixed the "gasifier" (German *Vergaser*); when he shifted gears, he pressed down the "klutsch" or the "cuppling" (German *Kuppelung*); and when people wanted gas, he "tanked" the car up with "benzene" (*Benzin* is gasoline in German). If my vocabulary in auto-mechanical matters failed me sometimes, I could always blame it on my German mechanic friend.

Many of the older generation were opposed to the newfangled, unbridled automobiles. Our neighbor Herr Standke called them brimstone-burning *Teufelswagen* ("Devil's wagons"). He and the older people lived in constant fear that one of these infernal horseless buggies would stampede their horses and wreck their vehicles. My father, too, was less than eager to buy a car. He had bought a fancy surrey recently and it had shiny wheels, leather-upholstered seats, coal-oil lamps, and tassels on the top. But the age of automobiles was upon us, and Father couldn't hold out long because the whole family put pressure on him and some of his friends led the way by buying their own motorized vehicles.

So he bought his first car in 1916. It was a four-door, black Dodge with high headlamps and demountable rims. Although the top could be folded back, we did not call the car a convertible. There were several elongated, pointed windows in the back, an easily recognizable hallmark of all Dodge cars in the teens. When it rained, we dug out the side curtains from their storage space under the backseat cushion. By the time we got the curtains up, we were thoroughly wet, but we kept the inside of the car dry.

When we got the car, Charlie Willmann, the agent who had sold it to us, agreed to teach my father how to drive. All went well as we chugged along the dirt highway. Charlie shifted gears while Father pushed in the clutch and pressed the "gas feeder." The sandy ruts were easy to follow, and my father was beginning to gain confidence until we approached a sharp right-angle turn. Charlie yelled at him to turn the wheel to the right. This made sense to Father because he was accustomed to pulling the right rein to make his horses turn right. So he turned the wheel, and the car obeyed just like his horses, but unlike his horses the car kept on going to the right and plowed into the fence. Charlie had failed to tell his pupil to turn back to the left to straighten out the car. Our horses did this as soon as you stopped pulling the right rein, but the car did not. This was more than Father had bargained for, and he refused to drive on. Charlie drove the car back home, and my older brothers took over the driving.

When we first got the car, I was still too small to drive, but I was enchanted by the prospects of driving. I dreamed of myself hurtling along country roads, surging around curves, roaring through sandy creeks, jerking the wheel to the right, to the left, snatching at quivering levers, stamping on jumping pedals, racing or calming a trembling motor, turning a gadget here, and grasping a knob there as I sped past gasping friends and rearing horses. Finally my mother made me a cushion that I placed behind my back so I could reach the pedals, and I learned to drive. However, there wasn't much hurtling along country roads and surging around curves. I had too much difficulty reaching the pedals and turning the big steering wheel.

Some years later I taught my father how to drive, which he did in his own fashion. While I was teaching him the fundamentals, I had frequent occasions to admonish him to step on the brake, and while he slowly made up his mind to do so, I pushed my feet ankle-deep into the floorboard. We had to remind him sometimes to shift gears when he drove too far and fast in low or second gear, which we called medium. He usually took off in a roar and with a sudden jerk. You could easily see where he had catapulted the vehicle forward because the wheels dug in the dirt where he launched the car. There may be some things I don't remember about my father, but I do know for sure that he was better at handling horses than at driving a car.

When we had only minor shopping to do and did not want to make the long trip to Mason, we shopped at the little country store at Plehweville, or Art. It was only two miles from home, and it had a post office. One item we bought here often was roasted coffee in bulk. Before the time when grocery stores and general merchandise stores installed coffee grinders with large brightly-colored wheels and handles, we bought whole, roasted coffee beans. Although the coffee aroma of the beans was not as great as the fragrance of grinding coffee and boiling it at home, there was a pleasant scent when the beans were poured out on the scales on the store counter, right before our eyes and under our noses. Later we bought our coffee in big red cans, probably Arbuckle or Star brand, and then we missed most of the coffee fragrance in the store.

There is no place on earth with the variety of smells that permeated the general merchandise stores in the country. The aroma of coffee was well mixed with all sorts of other smells oozing out from Duke's Mixture or Bull Durham smoking tobacco, from dried dill and pickles, dried apricots, peaches, and prunes, fresh apples, yellow cheese, soda crackers, vinegar, ginger, black pepper, flour, sugar, licorice sticks, gumdrops, peppermint, spices, extract of vanilla, ointments, and salves. Farther back in the store were some stray odors seeping out from bottles full of screwworm killer and liniment, drums of coal oil, turpentine, and linseed oil, as well as the smell of grass brooms, hemp rope, and leather goods.

Neither country stores nor mercantile establishments in town had as many paper sacks or bags as the stores do now. For this reason most of the merchandise was wrapped in paper and tied with twine or cord. The wrapping paper was kept handy on the counter in large, wide rolls. Desired lengths could be torn off by unrolling some of the paper and giving it a quick upward jerk against the heavy blade resting across the roll. Balls of cord were kept in metal dispensers on top of the paper holders. Some clerks were adept at tying a loop knot that could be easily untied at home so the cord could be saved. Others tied a hard square knot, but no matter how the cord was tied, we managed to remove it carefully at home and save it for future use.

My father usually bought his chewing tobacco at Dannheim's Store. While my mother or some other member of the family gathered up the coffee, vinegar, vaseline, and coal oil, Herr Dannheim took a big chunk of black Star-brand tobacco, pressed down the guillotine-like cutter, and chopped off several pieces, and my father left with several chunks of tobacco in his pockets. I was always glad when he bought Star-brand tobacco because he gave me the little metal stars, and I hammered them onto blocks of wood.

The little post office was crowded into the northwest corner of the store. We could transact normal post-office business there, but only when the store business did not occupy the owner. The usual procedure was to catch Mr. Dannheim, or one of his later successors, after he had squeezed himself into the tiny post-office cubicle and then ask him for our mail. There wasn't too much mail coming into our obscure community, but we had some relatives and friends who wrote periodically, and then there were the catalogues and packages from Sears, Roebuck and Montgomery Ward mail-order houses in Dallas and Fort Worth. The mail was brought in by large horse-drawn hacks or stagecoaches that made round trips between Mason and Llano every day. In addition to mail, they could carry a few passengers and trunks to or from the railroad terminal in Llano. At one time a four-span stagecoach ran between Mason and Burnet.

At this point I must pay a well-deserved tribute to the Post Office Department. In 1947 a distant relative, Karl Jordan of Bad Salzdetfurth in West Germany, being in great need because of Germany's defeat in World War II, wanted to write to his relatives in Texas to solicit food for his starving family. In his desperation he found some letters that my immigrant grandfather Ernst Jordan had written in 1889 and 1890 from Plehweville, Texas, to his relatives in Germany. So Karl wrote a letter to the descendants of Ernst Jordan in Plehweville; fortunately he added "Mason County" to the address, and the letter was delivered to Emil Jordan, one of the members of the family in Mason. It seems incredible that over a quarter of a century after the name "Plehweville" was dropped, a letter addressed to no one person in particular, only the descendants of a man who had died over fifty years earlier, was still delivered correctly. Of course, the addition of "Mason County" helped greatly, but even so it was a remarkable performance. Some years later Karl made handwritten copies of my grandfather's letters, and I have long treasured them.

As a result of his letter, Karl Jordan received abundant aid from his long-forgotten relatives in America. Several members of the Texas Jordans, who sent packages, made new acquaintances and became friends of the German Jordans. I myself have visited this family in Germany on four different trips abroad since 1950. Karl was ninety-seven years old when he died in 1978.

The coming of automobiles, trucks, and buses, decreasing the isolation of the countryside, has caused many rural communities to dwindle or die. They have already lost their schools by consolidation with the towns', and they are losing their country stores, post offices, and churches; even their homes are sometimes abandoned. The country people who have not moved to town now buy almost all their groceries—including meat, cheese, butter, milk, vegetables, and fruits—in supermarkets, just like the people in town. They depend on the big shippers and their trucks to keep them supplied not only with staple groceries but also with perishable meats and dairy products, as well as garden and orchard produce.

To be sure, there is a great new interest in country stores and rural communities, but this is mostly nostalgia and escapism on the part of city dwellers who don't have the slightest intention of returning to the earlier primitive life-style. And when real-estate developers build new rural communities and villages, they usually dig up the countryside and its trees and build roads and houses very similar to those the city dwellers left behind. For this reason it is especially refreshing to go to the genuine, old rural settlements and towns and try to recapture the life of an earlier day.

9

Hundred Years of
Texas German

Texas German is far removed, both in space and in character, from the central-European German from which it derived. Nevertheless, there are still far more similarities than differences between the two language groups. The basic structure is the same, but Texas German deviates in various ways from the mother tongue. Some of the differences are grammatical, especially in use of cases, but the greatest change in Texas German is in vocabulary and idiom.

The one hundred years, roughly 1845–1945, when Texas German developed and was in its prime were a century of tremendous change. The German settlers who came to Texas in the mid-1800's knew nothing about automobiles, trucks, tractors, road graders, airplanes, telephones, phonographs, radio, television, electric lights, batteries, and electric motors, because these modern inventions did not exist at that time. Consequently, the vast technological vocabulary and the everyday speech relating to these matters were unknown. Moreover, many of the words and idioms pertaining to ranching and to large-scale, Texas-style cattle raising were new, as were various school-game terms. When German settlers were faced with this new life and livelihood, they encountered the new situations primarily in English.

The result of this enormous bombardment of new technological and agricultural vocabulary was the extensive influx of English words into Texas German and the incorporation of many new expressions in everyday language. Meanwhile, the people in Germany experienced the same changes, indeed in some cases they produced them, and they coined a whole new vocabulary unknown to the isolated German settlers in Texas. So while Germany built up its new vocabulary in

Europe, the Texas Germans borrowed needed English terms, and hundreds of English words slipped in easily by default.

At first the borrowed words may have seemed somewhat foreign, but they were indispensable and soon were generally accepted and germanized. Ultimately the people could not differentiate in many cases between genuine German words and the Anglo borrowings. After all, there are thousands of related words that are quite similar in English and German, as for example: "the house" and *das Haus*, "the mouse" and *die Maus*, "the hand" and *die Hand*, "the shoulder" and *die Schulter*. For this reason the people soon felt the same relationship existed between "the rope" and *das Rope* (German *das Seil*), "the fence" and *die Fence* (German *der Zaun*), "the car" and *die Car* (German *der Wagen*).

In such cases as *das Rope* and *die Fence*, there were perfectly good German words available and known to the people, but they neglected them or failed to adapt them to the new situations, using instead the English terms. In most instances, however, the Texas Germans had no words at all for the new situations and things. In this respect they were linguistically impoverished in German. No wonder the English words were absorbed eagerly and quickly germanized, for example when English nouns were assigned German *die-der-das* gender. I have collected a list of nearly five-hundred English loanwords in Texas German. Here is a sampling of such words in technological matters: *der Blowout, die Exhaustpipe, der Gearshifter, greasen* ("to grease a car"), *der Monkeywrench, die Pliers, das Runningboard, der Sparkplug, das Steeringwheel*, and *der Windshieldwiper*. For farm and ranch life we might list the following words: *der Bollweevil, die Buggywhip, der Cornsheller, der Cowboy, die Crowbar, cultivaten* ("to cultivate"), *fencen* ("to fence"), *die Gate, die Gravelroad, die Hack, der Hatchet, der Maverick, der Outlaw, die Ranch*, and *der Roundup*. School-game terminology pertains mainly to baseball: *der Baseball* ("the ball"), *das Baseball* ("the game"), *batten* ("to bat"), *der Curve-ball, der Hit, der Homerun, der Pitcher*, and *sliden* ("to slide").

Compound nouns made up of German and English words are especially interesting. Good illustrations of such combinations are: *die Steinfence* ("the stone fence"), *die Riegelfence* ("the rail fence"), *die Stacheldrahtfence* ("the barbwire fence"), *das Butchermesser* ("the butcher knife"), *der Mesquitebaum* ("the mesquite tree"), *die Mehlbox* ("the flour box"), *die Sattelbags* ("the saddlebags"), *der Gummitire* ("the rubber tire"), *der Wassertank* ("the water tank"), *die Kuhpenne* ("the cowpen"), *die Schweinepenne* ("the pigpen"), *das Smokehaus* ("the smokehouse"), *der Feuercracker* ("the fire-cracker"), *die Eisenbahntracks* ("the railway tracks"), and *Zweibits* ("two bits").

There are also a number of mixed phrases, made up of German and English words, for instance: *Vieh dippen* ("to dip cattle"), *Vieh ropen* ("to rope cattle"), *Vieh aufrounden* ("to round up cattle"), *Wasser scrapen* ("to scrape water"), *Schweine butchern* ("to butcher hogs"), *die Kuh dehornen* ("to dehorn the cow"), *die Car aufjacken* ("to jack up the car"), *den Tire aufpumpen* ("to pump up the tire"), *die Wurst smoken* ("to smoke the sausage"), *zur Campmeeting gehen* ("to go to the camp meeting"), *die Car fahren* ("to drive the car"), *den Draht stretchen* ("to stretch the wire"), *mit dem Sixshooter schiessen* ("to shoot with the six-shooter"), and *das Feld einfencen* ("to fence in the field").

Borrowed verbs were always given regular principal parts in German and were conjugated like German verbs, for example: *cranken, crankte, habe gecrankt* ("crank, cranked, have cranked"). We would say: *Ich crank' die Car* ("I crank the car"), *Ich werde die Car cranken* ("I will crank the car"), and *Ich habe die Car gecrankt* ("I have cranked the car").

The speakers of Texas German were not much better off with their telephone terminology. Therefore, they borrowed English words and germanized them—for example, nouns like *der Receiver* and *die Central*, and verbs like *connecten* ("to connect") and *aufringen* ("to ring" or "to call up"). We would say: *Ich habe den Receiver aufgehängt* ("I have hung up the receiver"), *Ich habe meinen Freund aufgerungen* ("I have called up my friend"). Any German hearing the latter expression would be puzzled because he would hear: "I have wrung up my friend." Another amusing expression is: *Wir meeten* (German *treffen*) *uns heute in Town* ("We'll meet in town today"). Again a German would misunderstand completely because he would hear: *Wir mieten uns heute in Town* ("We'll rent each other in town today") and he would have no idea what the word *Town* meant.

There are a number of similar expressions or idioms in Texas

German that most Germans would find hilariously funny or that would be totally beyond their comprehension. Here are some such expressions: *Ich habe die Kuh geropt* ("I've roped the cow"); *Die Kuh ist über die Fence gejumpt* ("The cow jumped over the fence"); *Das hat mich aber getickelt* ("That really tickled [amused] me"); *Wir haben eine gute Zeit gehabt* ("We had a good time"); *Das ist sure interessant* ("That surely is interesting"); *Das beat doch alles* ("That really beats everything"). In the last case above a German would think the speaker was saying: *Das biet't doch alles* ("That really offers everything").

When German Texans coined a German word from an English one, they usually retained the English pronunciation, but in many cases there would be a distinct German flavor and a strong German intonation. When a German Texan borrowed *smokehouse*, the German version came out as *Schmokehaus*, and *cotton* was pronounced *Kutton*. *Steeringwheel* would be *Schtieringviel*, *sparkplug* became *Schparkpluk*, and *store* was pronounced *Schtohr*.

The pronunciation of standard German words resembled the sound system in Germany, but certain peculiarities became more prominent in Texas than in Europe. Umlaut distinctions were generally ignored. Consequently, *ä* became *e* (*spät* pronounced *spet*, "late"), *ö* became *e* (*schön* pronounced *schen*, "beautiful"), *ü* became *i* (*kühl* pronounced *kihl*, "cool"). The letter *r* was either trilled, as in *treu* ("true"), or it was lost completely, so that *lieber Bruder* ("dear brother") came out as *lieba Bruda*; Ernst Jordan's name sounded like *Enst Yoddan*; *fahren* ("to drive") was simply *fahn*; *Geburtstag* ("birthday") was pronounced *Gebutstag*; and *schwarz* ("black") became *schwatz*.

As the German Texans learned to speak English, certain familiar sounds were carried over into the new language, and an unmistakable German accent became normal in the pronunciation of English among the German settlers. This can still be heard most clearly in the pronunciation of certain consonants. In general, the final *b*, *d*, and *g* were hardened in English, as they are in German. Thus words like *rob*, *barb*, and *rib* were pronounced *rop*, *barp*, and *rip*, for example: "He broke a *rip* venn he fell." The words *hand*, *land*, and *had* became *hant*, *lant*, and *hat*, as in "I *hat* a sore *hant*." A similar hardening occurred in the final *g* in words like *dog*, *hog*, and *log*, so they sounded like *dok*, *hok*, and *lok*: "He hat a goot *hok dok*."

Also the final and intermediate *th* sounds hardened into a *t*. In these cases *both* became *bot*; *bother*, *botter*; and *nothing*, *notting*. The initial *th* sound caused much trouble and frequently resulted in a *d*—for example, *dat* for *that*, *denn* for *then*, *dere* for *there*, and *dirty* for *thirty*. A similar problem was presented by the initial *w* and *wh*, which became *v* sounds among some German Texans in words like *vas* for *was*, *vindow* for *window*, *visky* for *whisky*, and *vork* for *work*.

The *s* sound at the beginning of words caused something of a problem. Many people voiced this *s* sound as in German *sein* (pronounced *zine*), and the sound came out regularly as an English *z*. Thus *sink* became *zink*, *see* was pronounced *zee*, and *salt* sounded like *zalt*. A very common variant was heard in the pronunciation of the initial *sm*, *sp*, and *st*. As in German, the *s* in these combinations was pronounced as *sch* (English *sh*), and this resulted in pronunciations like *schmall*, *schmear*, *schmoke*; *schpeak*, *schpit*, *schpook*; and *schtiff*, *schtore*, and *schtorm*. For example, they would say, "Dey *schtayt* in de olt house to zee dat *schpook*" ("They stayed in the old house to see that spook").

Some German idioms were translated literally into English, and these expressions add a special flavor to the English of German Texans. When you hear someone say "The bread is all" (German *Das Brot ist alle*), he means "The bread is all gone."

Texas German is still spoken in parts of the Texas Hill Country. If you keep your ears pricked and are lucky, you might hear some unusual stories in the German settlements because the German-English bilingualism produced several interesting anecdotes based upon slight misunderstandings. The widely circulated tale about Sheriff Klaerner, the elder, of Fredericksburg is one such story. The sheriff, who was well liked and admired by the people, let it be known that he had a horse for sale. When an Anglo buyer came and saw the horse, he said, "That's a good horse; I'll buy him." Said Sheriff Klaerner, "But I must tell you, dat horse don't look goodt." "Looks good to me," said the man; "I'll take him." And he paid for the horse and rode off proudly, leading the strong, sleek horse. A week later he brought back the horse and said: "Say, Herr Klaerner, that horse is blind and can't see a darn thing. I want my money back." "I tolt you dat horse don't look goodt," replied Klaerner.

Another story based on a misunderstanding tells about a Texas-German widow who ordered a tombstone for the grave of her departed husband. She wanted the inscription to read *Ruhe sanft* ("Rest in peace"), and she wanted it on both sides of the stone (*auf beiden Seiten*). The stonecutter, who was not completely conversant with German, wrote down a memo for himself and in a few days proceeded to carve the epitaph on the stone. Some months later the memorial was finished and set up in the usual fashion with its newly engraved inscription. When the widow came to inspect the headstone, the carver proudly showed her the engraving, but the lady was astounded at the sight of the epitaph, which read: *Ruhe sanft auf beiden Seiten.*

Even the few blacks in the Hill Country spoke German, and they identified more with the German Texans than they did with the Anglos. The story is told about one such black who knew German so well that he could speak it in dialect form. During World War I, when German Texans were persecuted and hounded for their German ancestry and language, the black German Texan spoke up in German dialect and told his fellow townsmen on the streets of Fredericksburg, "Mir Deutscha müssa zusamasticka" (*Wir Deutschen müssen zusammenhalten*: "We Germans must stick together").

Our German neighbor Hermann Standke also had an amusing misunderstanding once, when he was peddling a tow sack full of large and small chickens in town. Mr. J. W. White, the rich Anglo banker and the prospective buyer, who could not speak or understand German well, said, "Most of those fryers are good, and I'll take them, but two are too small." Now the English word *small* is etymologically related to the German word *schmal*, and it is pronounced similarly, but the German word means "narrow." When Mr. Standke heard that two of his chickens were too "narrow" (*schmal*), his Teutonic temper flared, and he proclaimed indignantly in his Swabian-German dialect that those two chickens were just as *breit* ("broad") as the rest, only a bit *klein* ("small").

The German Hill Country of Mason County still abounds in typical German family names. There are Arhelgers, Bernhards, Bickenbachs, Brandenbergers, Dannheims, Ellebrachts, Geistweidts, Hasses, Hoersters, Hofmanns, Kellers, Kothmanns, Lehmanns, Lehmbergs, Lemburgs, Metzgers, Muellers, Reichenaus, Schmidts, Schoenfelds, Splittgerbers, Wartenbachs, Willmanns, Wissemanns, and hundreds of others. Changes have been extremely rare. I know of only one certain translation locally, and that is the one from Fuchs to Fox. Long, difficult names were occasionally shortened, like Sassmannshausen to Sassmann, but most of the difficult names have remained unchanged, for example, Schmidzensky. There was some anglicizing in the spelling, like transcribing the *ä*, *ö*, and *ü* to *ae*, *oe*, and *ue*: Schäfer to Schaefer, Löffler to Loeffler, and Schüssler to Schuessler. Also some people with names ending in the suffix *-mann* dropped the final *n*: Wiedeman.

German place names still exist throughout the German Belt of Texas. In the Hill Country, the names of three county seats are German: Boerne (Kendall County), Fredericksburg (Gillespie County), and New Braunfels (Comal County). In addition to these larger towns, there are many small communities and villages with German names. In Bexar County we have places like Elmendorf and St. Hedwig; in Comal County, Anhalt, Fischer, Gruene, Startzville, and Sattler; in Gillespie County, Mecklenburg, Eckert, and Luckenbach; in Guadalupe County, Barbarosa, New Berlin, Schertz, Weinert, Zorn, and Zuehl; in Kendall County, Bergheim and Kreuzberg; in Llano County, Castell; and in Mason County, Hedwigs Hill and Hilda. Many of the original German immigrants established small rural settlements, but most of these have disappeared, and some have been renamed. In Mason County alone there were at least five such places, and all had the suffix *-ville* added to family names: Bodeville, Grossville, Hoersterville, Plehweville, and Simonville.

German has remained common in Texas, but it has undergone great changes. This is particularly true of vocabulary and idioms. This change came about by extensive borrowing and germanizing of English words and expressions. In pronunciation as well as in the meaning of words, there was considerable cross-influence between English and German, resulting sometimes in funny situations, anecdotes, and folk tales.

Afterword

THEY are still standing there by the Willow Creek: my parental home, the Methodist Church, the little school, and the store. Their days are numbered, though, and some are already deserted and idle. The church is still active, but it is one of only four remaining churches of the original eight German Methodist congregations in the Llano Valley. Many of the rural people of my days are dead, others have moved to the cities and towns, and some of the descendants of the German settlers have intermingled with other ethnic groups and thus helped to form the great American melting pot.

Five of my brothers and sisters are still living, but none resides in the countryside anymore. Almost all the farms are gone, but the ranches are thriving, perhaps more than ever, somewhat deserted, to be sure, because fewer and fewer ranchmen live on isolated homesteads. They have moved to town and tend their herds by pickups and have their livestock hauled to auction barns and feedlots in gigantic trailer trucks.

By these changes and by the rapid spread of the big cities into rural areas, the features of rural life in the Hill Country are being eroded. And now the Germanness of the German Belt is further threatened by engulfment in a powerful wave of Hispanic-American newcomers. These changes together are taking a heavy toll from the formerly isolated German settlements.

In spite of these changes, however, much of the nineteenth-century German cultural heritage still remains and will continue to live on for many years. The church, now amalgamated with Anglo Methodism, is still viable, although some of the members live in town and commute to the country for Sunday services. The German language is still spoken here and there, especially among the older generation, but it has decreased greatly in use and purity. German character traits like thoroughness, determination, and reliability will live on as long as the descendants of the German settlers live in the Hill Country. Also the German work ethic, the love of land, the patriotism and loyalty to our country, and the joy of song and music will remain active as indigenous virtues and values.

Fortunately, a new impetus to the preservation of the various cultures of our state has come from a recently awakened concern over the state's diverse ethnic groups and their contributions to our common cultural heritage. This can be seen in various books and publications, in symposiums on ethnic contributions, in museums, and in the Institute of Texan Cultures in San Antonio. All these influences will work for the prolongation and, it is hoped, for the perpetuation of the diverse cultures, including the German. It is the author's hope that the present book will contribute to this new trend.

Bibliography

Alexander, Drury B. *Texas Homes of the Nineteenth Century*. Austin: University of Texas Press, 1966.

Bacon, Paul Valentine. *New German Grammar for Beginners*. Boston: Allyn and Bacon, 1916.

Bierschwale, Margaret. "Mason County, Texas, 1845–1870." *The Southwestern Historical Quarterly* 52 (April, 1949): 379–397.

Biesele, Rudolph L. *The History of the German Settlements in Texas, 1831–1861*. Austin: von Boeckmann-Jones, 1930.

Bones, Jim, Jr., and John Graves. *Texas Heartland: A Hill Country Year*. College Station: Texas A&M University Press, 1975.

A Century of German Methodism in the Llano River Valley of Texas, 1852–1952: History and Pageant. Fredericksburg, Texas: privately printed, 1952.

Douglass, Paul F[ranklin]. *The Story of German Methodism: Biography of an Immigrant Soul*. New York: The Methodist Book Concern, 1939.

Eikel, Fred, Jr. "New Braunfels German." *American Speech* 41 (February, 1966): 5–16; (December, 1966): 254–260; and 42 (May, 1967): 83–104.

Eilers, Kathryn Burford. "A History of Mason County." Master's thesis, University of Texas, Austin, 1939.

Ellis, L. Tuffly, Terry G. Jordan, and James R. Buchanan. *Cultural and Historical Maps of Texas*. Austin: The University of Texas, Bureau of Business Research, 1976. Originally published as part of *Atlas of Texas*, edited by Stanley A. Arbingast et al. Austin: The University of Texas, Bureau of Business Research, 1976.

Estill, Julia. "Customs among the German Descendants of Gillespie County." In *The Folklore of Texan Cultures*, edited by Francis Edward Abernethy, pp. 145–151. Austin: The Encino Press, 1974.

Fischer, Dan, comp. *The Willmanns in Texas, 1853–1953*. Privately printed, [1953?].

Flach, Vera. *A Yankee in German America: Texas Hill Country*. San Antonio: Naylor, 1973.

Gilbert, Glenn G. "English Loanwords in the German of Fredericksburg, Texas." *American Speech* 40 (May, 1965): 102–112.

Gillespie County Historical Society, ed. and comp. *Pioneers in God's Hills: A History of Fredericksburg and Gillespie County People and Events.* 2 vols. Austin: von Boeckmann-Jones, 1960, 1974.

Grote, Charles H. *The History of the German Methodist Episcopal Church, South, Organized by Rev. Chas. A. Grote at Castell, Llano County, Texas, March 8, 1856.* [Fredericksburg, Texas]: privately printed, 1931.

―――. "Kurze geschichtliche Notizen der Llano Gemeinde." *Der Missionsfreund* 36 (July 2, 1931): 2 ff.

Johnson, Charles A. *The Frontier Camp Meeting: Religious Harvest Time.* Dallas: Southern Methodist University Press, 1955.

Jordan, Ervin M. "The Work of the Methodist Episcopal Church, South, among the Germans in Texas." Master's thesis, Southern Methodist University, 1935.

Jordan Gilbert J. "The Texas German Language of the Western Hill Country." *Rice University Studies* 63 (Summer, 1977): 59–71.

―――. "Texas German Methodism in a Rural Setting." *Perkins Journal* 31 (Spring, 1978): 1–21.

Jordan, Gilbert J., and Terry G. Jordan. *Ernst and Lisette Jordan: German Pioneers in Texas.* Austin: von Boeckmann-Jones, 1971.

Jordan, Terry G. "The German Element in Texas: An Overview." *Rice University Studies* 63 (Summer, 1977): 1–11.

―――. *German Seed in Texas Soil: Immigrant Farmers in Nineteenth-Century Texas.* Austin: University of Texas Press, 1966.

―――. "The German Settlements in Texas after 1865." *The Southwestern Historical Quarterly* 73 (October, 1969): 193–212.

―――. "The Old-World Antecedent of the Fredericksburg Easter Fires." In *The Folklore of Texan Cultures*, edited by Francis Edward Abernethy, pp. 151–156. Austin: The Encino Press, 1974.

―――. "The Patterns of Origins of the *Adelsverein* German Colonists." *Texana* 6 (Fall, 1968): 245–257.

King, Irene Marschall. *John O. Meusebach: German Colonizer in Texas.* Austin: University of Texas Press, 1967.

Kniffen, Fred B. "Milestones and Stumbling Blocks." *Pioneer America* 7 (January, 1975): 2.

Lee, Umphrey. *The Lord's Horseman: John Wesley the Man.* New York and London: The Century Company, 1928. Republished in Nashville by The Abington Press, 1954.

Liebhart, H[einrich], ed. *Liederlust und Psalter-Harfe mit Anhang.* Cincinnati, 1876.

Magaret, E. O., ed., and George J. Meyer, collector. *Die Kleine Palme.* Chicago: Meyer and Brothers, no date.

Mason County Historical Commission and the Mason County Historical Society, comps. *Mason County Historical Book*. Mason, Texas: privately printed, 1976.

Mason County News (Mason, Texas), various volumes, including 1903, 1909, 1912, 1924, 1952, and 1953.

The Methodist Hymnal. Nashville: The Methodist Publishing House, 1968.

Nail, Olin W., ed. *Texas Methodist Centennial Yearbook, 1834–1934*. Elgin, Texas: privately printed, 1934.

Nast, Wilhelm, and Heinrich Liebhart, eds. *Deutsches Gesang- und Melodienbuch der Bischöflichen Methodistenkirche*. Cincinnati: Curts & Jannings, 1888. There are many other editions.

————, eds. *Gesangbuch der Bischöflichen Methodisten Kirche*. Nashville and Dallas: Publishing House of the Methodist Episcopal Church, South, 1910.

Olmsted, Frederick Law. *A Journey through Texas*. New York: Dix, Edwards, 1857. Reprinted in Austin by the University of Texas Press, 1978.

Owens, William A. *A Fair and Happy Land*. New York: Scribners, 1975.

————. "The Play Party in Texas." Master's thesis, Southern Methodist University, 1933.

————. *This Stubborn Soil*. New York: Scribners, 1966.

Penniger, Robert, ed. *Fest-Ausgabe zum 50-Jährigen Jubiläum der Gründung der Stadt Friedrichsburg*. Fredericksburg, Texas: Fredericksburger Wochenblatt, 1896. Also published in translation as *The First Fifty Years*. Translated by Charles L. Wisseman. Fredericksburg, Texas: Fredericksburg Publishing Co., 1971.

Polk, Stella Gipson. *Mason and Mason County*. Austin: The Pemberton Press, 1966.

Radetzky, F. W. "Kurzer geschichtlicher Bericht des Deutschen Werkes der Südlichen Methodisten-Kirche in Texas." *Der Missionsfreund* 36 (January 22, 1932): 1–4.

Sankey, Ira D., James McGranahan, and George C. Stebbins. *Church Hymns and Gospel Songs*. New York: Biglow and Main, 1887.

Schiwetz, E. M. *Buck Schiwetz' Texas*. Austin: University of Texas Press, 1960.

Schmidt, Bruno C. "A History of the Southern Conference." Master's thesis, Southern Methodist University, 1935.

Schmidt, Curt E. *Opa and Oma: German-Texas Pioneers*. New Braunfels, Texas: Folkways Publishing Company, 1975.

Service Book and Hymnal of the Lutheran Church in America. Edited by the Commission on Liturgy and the Commission on the Hymnal. Minneapolis: Fortress, 1958.

Washburn, Charles C., ed. *The New Cokesbury Hymnal*. Nashville: The Cokesbury Press, 1928.

Weilbacher, A. "Zubereitung von Wein aus der Mustang-Traube." *Schütze's Jahrbuch für Texas . . . für 1884.* Austin: A. Schütze, 1883.

Wilson, Joseph B. "The German Language in Central Texas Today." *Rice University Studies* 63 (Summer, 1977): 47–58.

————. "The Texas Germans of Lee and Washington Counties." *Rice University Studies* 47 (Winter, 1960): 83–98.

Index

Abendglocken, 74

agriculture. *See* farming; gardening; ranching

Anglo Texans: attitudes of, toward Germans, 14–16, 100, 137; influence of, on German customs, 56, 89, 124–127, 133–135; as members of German communities, 98–99, 140–141

animals: anecdotes about, 19–20, 65; care of, 26–27, 30–31, 60, 62–63, 67, 68; commercial uses of, 63, 64, 65, 66; domestic uses of, 31, 48–49, 50–52, 66; in farming and ranching, 30, 64, 65–66, 68; as pets, 19–20, 63, 65, 66; wild, 19, 70–72, 108. *See also* cattle; hogs; horses

architecture, 143; examples of, 73–74, 96, 115, 143–144; of Jordan homes, 6, 19–26

Art (Tex.) (Plehweville, Upper Willow Creek, *Oberwillow Creek*): church buildings in, 13, 94; education in, 96–116; folklore in, 34–36, 101–103, 105–107, 128–135; German people in, 3–4, 6, 8–10, 13–19, 38, 73, 81–82, 87, 89, 97–98, 136; houses in, 19, 144; Methodists in, 9, 10, 13, 73–95; Mexicans in, 98; name of, 12; post office in, 13–14, 149–151; ranching in, 6, 12–14, 17, 26, 29–31, 55–71; stores in, 13–14, 149–151

automobiles: attitudes toward, 148; effects of, on customs, 138, 146–148, 151; Father and, 29, 148–149; garages and mechanics for, 146–148; Model T, 99–100, 137

banks, 140–141

Bible, 21, 33, 85–86; as award, 85; Martin Luther version of, 81; memory verses from, 84, 85; in religious services, 78–79, 81, 88, 92, 94; verses from, on tombstones, 94

Bible school, 74, 85, 95

Bickenbach, Daniel, 6, 60

Bickenbach, Friederika, 6

Bickenbach, Lisette (Mrs. Ernst Jordan), 5–6, 9, 16

Bickenbach, Peter, 6, 9

Bickenbach, Sophie Willach, 6

Bickenbach, Wilhelm, 6

Bickenbach family, 5, 6–7, 9

birds, 71, 103, 104, 108

blacksmiths, 145–146

Blinn College (Brenham, Tex.), 97

Blue Mountain ranch, 120, 140

boots, 71, 139–140

box supper, 99

bread, 4–5, 39–40, 44

buffalo, 70–71

buggies, 75, 109, 137, 142

cactus, 13, 61–62

camp meetings, 89–93

cards, 125–126

Castell (Tex.), 9, 10, 23, 96

Catholic church, 8, 73

cats, 19–20, 31, 66

cattle, 4, 5, 6, 8, 13, 67; accidents involving, 57–59; branding of, 60, 62; breeds of, 55; dipping of, 57; doctoring of, 56, 59–60; drives of, 6, 61; feeding of, 26–27, 30, 61–62, 68; grass for, 13, 26, 61; inspection of, 56; roping of, 57–58; roundups of, 6, 56; water for, 61, 67

cellar, 25

cemeteries, 94–95

cheese, 38, 40–41, 50, 110

Cherokee Junior College, 98